Emmanuelle Vaugier 56 Success Fa

Everything You Need To Know About Emmanuelle Vaugier

Contents

Saw II - Plot

List of Saw characters#Michael Marks|Michael Marks (Noam Jenkins), a police force informer, wakes up to notice a spike-filled disguise sealed about his nape. A tape as of Jigsaw (Saw)|Jigsaw notifies him that he has one minute to get back the key as of beyond his right eye with a SCALPEL, however he can't carry him self to undertake thus and is slayed once the disguise shuts on his head. Detective List of Saw characters#Eric Matthews|Eric Matthews (Donnie Wahlberg) is afterward named to the set by Detective List of Saw characters#Allison Kerry|Allison Kerry (Dina Meyer) once she uncovers a communication for him. Initially unwilling to come to be included with the situation, Eric chooses to unite Kerry and the police force in directing a SWAT group to an deserted steel plant. Here they notice Jigsaw (Saw)|John Kramer (Tobin Bell), whoever is feeble as of malignancy, as well like computer screens displaying 8 folks, containing List of Saw characters#Daniel Matthews|Daniel (Erik Knudsen), Eric's boy, and Amanda Young (Shawnee Smith), the solely familiar toughie of John's diversions. They are altogether confined inner a home and have 2 hours beforehand a nervus go-between stuffing the home executes them, however John guarantees Eric that he must notice his boy in a secure, safe state if he plainly chats with John only. With a few force as of Kerry, Eric unwillingly concurs in line to purchase time for the police force technology group to turn up and trail the wave as of the home.

The 8 sufferers - Daniel, Amanda, List of Saw characters#Gus Colyard|Gus (Tony Nappo), List of Saw characters#Obi Tate|Obi (Timothy Burd), List of Saw characters#Xavier Chavez|Xavier (Franky G), List of Saw characters#Laura Hunter|Laura (Beverley Mitchell), List of Saw characters#Jonas Singer|Jonas (Glenn Plummer), and List of Saw characters#Addison Corday|Addison (Emmanuelle Vaugier) - are informed by micro-cassette recorder that antidotes are concealed all over the home. One cure is in the secure, the amalgamation is in the back of their brains and the direction may be noticed over the rainbow. Despite a cautioning record, they aim to employ a key to leave the area, and Gus is shot lamented by the booby-trapped entrance as they aim to leave the area. After the timer ends the entrance opens and they create their means via the home and to the cellar, wherever it is disclosed that Obi aided abduct the other ones, that is maintained by Laura once she recollects her hijacking. Obi fain accesses the furnace to get back 2 antidotes, however the furnace activates as he attempts to get back the second and he is scorched living alongside with the antidotes beforehand the other ones may aid him. They resume sensing about,

and Jonas guides them to a area upfloors that Xavier and Addison split in to , that lodges an cure beyond a steel entrance and a needle-filled hole holding the key. The trial is denoted for Xavier, however he hurls Amanda in to the hole instead; although she recovers the key, Xavier nose-dives to undo the entrance in time and renounces the cluster out of exasperation.

Meanwhile, John progresses the 2 hours with chat either inactive and arcane with an progressively irritated Eric. During their chat it is rvealed that Eric was at one point a extremely esteemed official expected to his cruel and merciless style to police force work, however at the moment cowers beyond a bureau, and has a flunking connection with his former wife and boy. He finally divulges that following educating that he had malignancy, he attempted to effect self-murder by powering his automobile off a precipice, however outlived the smash notwithstanding his wounds, and noticed a spic-and-span account for existence. He additionally determined to trial the will to live of these whoever take their lives for given, with the time he had left. John The technology group comes, and John divulges that altogether of the present game's sufferers away as of Daniel remained framed by Eric for different offenses, delivering police force files like proof, and if his ID is ascertained, Daniel must be in hazard. At Kerry's proposal, Eric demolishes some files and sketches about the zone, although John states that he does not heed and it must not retain Eric's boy.

Xavier returns to the foremost area, wherever he uncovers a chromatic numeral on Gus's nape and registers that one numeral as of the amalgamation to the secure is authored in colored ink on the back of every one of their necks. Now despairing to get the cure, he executes Jonas in a brawl and starts hunting the other ones. Laura yields to the nervus go-between, experiencing been further influenced compared to the other ones, and Amanda and Addison either renouce Daniel following educating that Eric is his dad, although Amanda returns following detecting Jonas's form. Addison discovers a area with an cure in a glass container, however like she tries to get back it her arms come to be confined in the razor blade-lined sockets, and Xavier departs her to perish following perusing her numeral. With Xavier very warm on their rear, Amanda and Daniel return to the foremost area and notice a tunnel that guides to the Saw (2004 film)|abandoned amenities, holding Lawrence Gordon (Saw)|Lawrence Gordon's cut off base and the broken down principals of List of Saw characters#Adam Stanheight|Adam Stanheight and List of Saw characters#Zep Hindle|Zep Hindle. Daniel falls down inner simply beforehand Xavier discovers them. Amanda details out that he can't interpret his personal numeral, however Xavier cuts the epidermis as of his nape. He additionally advances to eliminate them, and Daniel gashes his nape with a Hacksaw, experiencing affected cave in.

Having noticed Xavier chasing Daniel via the home, Eric snaps and attacks John and drives him to take him to the home at gunpoint. The sitting zone they remained in revolves out to be a raise, that they employ to leave the plant. The SWAT group concurrently accesses a alike, however dissimilar home utilizing the audiovisual feed's wave however solely discovers VCRs performing formerly recorded pictures, disclosing that the happenings in the gas home took place beforehand they noticed John. The factory's timer ends and a great secure opens, inner that Kerry discovers Daniel confined and breathing in to an oxygen disguise. Unaware of whatever of this, Eric comes at the home, leaving John external. He finally finds the amenities, wherever he is striked by a pig-masked figure, and wakes up to notice him self shackled at the ankle joint to the pipes, and a micro-cassette recorder beside him that divulges that Amanda has come to be John's Protégé. She shows in the access and seals the amenities entrance, leaving Eric to perish. Outside, John perceives his shrieks and gradually forms a beam.

Higher Ground (TV series) - Reoccurring characters

* Brittney Irvin as Jess, Shelby's junior sister
* Lynda Boyd as Jess and Shelby's mother
* Jim Byrnes (actor)|Jim Byrnes as Frank, whoever set up Horizon following his boy Tom effected suicide
* Sean Campbell (actor)|Sean Campbell as Sheriff Curtis Swann whoever often assists the Cliffhangers and has a connection with Annie
* Benita Ha as Annie, whoever possesses the native eatery and lives with her 5-year-old girl Gracie
* Garwin Sanford as Martin Barringer, Scott's father
* **Emmanuelle Vaugier as Elaine Barringer, Scott's harmful stepmother**
* Kyle Alisharan as Hank, Kat's boyfriend
* Terence Kelly as Peter Scarbrow's dad, whoever passes away of a heart assault and departs Peter sufficient cash to purchase Horizon.
* C. Tutt as prospective vacationer

House of the Dead 2 (film) - Cast

* **Emmanuelle Vaugier as Dr. Alexandra/Alex 'Nightingale' Morgan**
* Ed Quinn as Lt. Ellis
* Sticky Fingaz as Dalton
* Steve Monroe as O'Conner
* Victoria Pratt as Henson
* James Parks (actor)|James Parks Bart (as James Jean Parks)
* Billy Brown (actor)|Billy Brown as Griffin
* Nadine Velazquez as Rodriguez

* Mircea Monroe as Sarah Curtis
* Ellie Cornell as Jordan Casper
* Jonathan Cherry as Rudy Curien (archives)
* Danielle Burgio as Alicia/Patient Zero (archives)
* Sid Haig as Professor Curien

Dolan's Cadillac (film) - Cast

* Wes Bentley as Tom Robinson
* Christian Slater as Jimmy Dolan
    * **Emmanuelle Vaugier as Elizabeth Robinson**
* Greg Bryk as Chief
* Aidan Devine as Roman
* Al Sapienza as Fletcher
* Karen LeBlanc as Delta
* Cory Generoux as Pedro
* Vivian Ng as Jun Li
* Patrick Bird as Jose
* Eugene Clark (actor)|Eugene Clark as Tink
* Max Keene as Danny
* Robert Benz as Sheriff Bob
* Timothy Allen as Marshall
* Amy Matysio as Amy
* Tony Munch as Blocker
* Darla Biccum as Reba

Magee Secondary School - Notable alumni

*Gary Basaraba - performer Brooklyn South, Boomtown
*Gil Bellows (1984), performer (with Morgan Freeman in The Shawshank Redemption; with Calista Flockhart in Ally McBeal)
*Robert Christy (1932) physicist
*Judy Chu Chun-chun (1998), actress
*Thomas Fung, media cluster originator - Fairchild Group
*Bruce Greenwood (1974), actor
*Margot Kidder (1965), female actor (with Christopher Reeve in Superman; with Robert Redford in The Great Waldo Pepper)
*Michelle Lang (1993), solely Canadian correspondent to perish in the War in Afghanistan (2001-present)|War in Afghanistan.
*Graham Ludlow (1979), performer, scriptwriter and maker (She Drives Me Crazy - Gemini Award for Best TV Movie - 2010)
*Grant McCracken (1969), Cultural Anthropologist

*Rebecca Marino, tennis player
*Scott Masse - with Bryan Hoad, 501 productions
*Carrie-Anne Moss (1985), female actor (with Keanu Reeves in The Matrix; with Guy Pearce in Memento)
*Grace Park (actress)|Grace Park (1992), model/actress (Battlestar Galactica, Hawaii Five-0)
*Justin Peck, Phantom of the Opera, New York and Hamburg http://www.thephantomoftheopera.com/new-york-people/cast/justin-peck
*Josh Ramsay (1998), head vocalist of the group Marianas Trench
*Dal Richards, Order of British Columbia|OBC conductor and musician
*Rachel Roberts (model)|Rachel Roberts (1996), female actor,model 2000 SI swimsuit edition
*Jeremy Ten (2008), figure skater, 2009 Canadian Bronze Medalist

***Emmanuelle Vaugier (b.1976), female actor (Two and a Half Men, Saw serials, with Josh Hartnett in 40 Days and 40 Nights, One Tree Hill, CSI: NY)**

*Matt Webb, guitar player of the group Marianas Trench (band)|Marianas Trench
*So You Think You Can Dance (season 7)#Alex Wong|Alex Wong, So You Think You Can Dance Season 6 (2010)
*Richard 'Disco Dick' Zokol- ex-PGA journey associate

Suddenly Naked - Cast

* Wendy Crewson - Jackie York
* Peter Coyote - Lionel
* **Emmanuelle Vaugier - Lupe Martinez**
* Joe Cobden - Patrick McKeating
* Jud Tylor - Crystal
* Jennifer Carmichael - Rainbow
* Eliza Murbach - Kelly
* Dan Joffre - Fan
* Camille Mitchell - Sasha
* Michael Shanks - Danny Blair
* Ron Selmour - Security Guard

Supernatural (season 2) - Casting

The authors applied the second season to enlarge on the idea of huntsmen, ensuing in the start of numerous repeating types via the hunter-frequented saloon—Harvelle's Roadhouse. Samantha Ferris pictured Ellen Harvelle, owner of the Roadhouse and an aged pal of John Winchester (Supernatural)|John Winchester, when Alona Tal played Ellen's girl Jo Harvelle|Jo. This couple accompanied the father-son connection of the Winchesters in the foremost annum.Knight, p.15 Ferris understands she was precisely what the creators remained sensing for: a hard, forceful, up till now a itty-bitty motherly performer.Knight, p.134 Tal's type, on the other side, was an designed fancy attention for Dean, and was finally staged out since she appeared off as further of a female sibling figure. Chad Lindberg pictured the mastermind Characters of Supernatural#Ash|Ash, whoever utilizes his huge computer expertises to trail the supernatural. Because the authors sensed the character's funny and bizarre character was also impractical for the show, he was as well eliminated by the climax.Knight, p.16

Other types restored as of the foremost annum. Actor Jim Beaver produced numerous emergences as huntsman Bobby Singer, an aged kin pal of the Winchesters. Beaver had anticipated his first-season visitor emergence in Devil's Trap to be a one-shot transact, and was startled once he was questioned to dispersed.Knight, p.136 Adrianne Palicki repeated her part as Sam's dead sweetheart Characters of Supernatural#Jessica Lee Moore|Jessica in the alternate-reality chapter What Is and What Should Never Be (Supernatural)|What Is and What Should Never Be, as did Samantha Smith as Mary Winchester (Supernatural)|Mary Winchester. Smith as well produced an emergence in a flashback in the penultimate chapter, All Hell Breaks Loose (Supernatural)|All Hell Breaks Loose, Part One. And although at foremost unwilling since of his part on Grey's Anatomy, Jeffrey Dean Morgan restored as John Winchester (Supernatural)|John Winchester in the season opening and climax. However, the type passes away in the opening since the authors fretted that experiencing him detached as of his boys again—Sam and Dean expend a lot of the foremost season trailing him down—would cut the show by experiencing him off undertaking further absorbing items compared to the lads are undertaking. As a devil, the baddie Azazel (Supernatural)|Azazel sporadically controls holds, and was foremost completely pictured by Morgan in the first-season climax. The restrains progressed to Fredric Lehne for the second-season opening, and the show's creators relished his execution thus a lot they accompanied him back for the two-part climax.

Many circumstances proceeded in to the directing resolutions of the season's visitor stars. Linda Blair, well known for her part in the terror feature The Exorcist (film)|The Exorcist, emerged in the chapter The Usual Suspects. Though a fan of the show, Blair had turned down a visitor emergence in the foremost season since she did not desire to dispersed to terror, experiencing consumed annums getting a spotless slate. This altered following the TV serials Extra (TV program)|Extra screened a three-part outline on her performing vocation and work with creatures. It endeavored to notice a serials that ought to record a part for her as an actor's bit, somewhat compared to a appearance. Kripke, a fan of The Exorcist,Knight, p.51 presented to record an chapter especially for her, and she was actually affected once he paid attention to her appeal to leave out devils in the plot line. During Dubbing (filmmaking)#ADR.2Fpost-sync|automated conversation substitution, Jensen Ackles appended in a mention to The Exorcist with the declaration, I might actually proceed for a few pea brume.Knight, pp.52–53

The directing of Battlestar Galactica (2004 TV series)|Battlestar Galactica Tricia Helfer in Roadkill stemmed as of the producers' partiality to employ performers essential to Supernatural fanbase. This was the foremost chapter to have the Winchesters as helping types, and Kripke sensed Tricia had the charm to accomplish the directing part.Knight, pp.89–90 Kripke relished Emmanuelle Vaugier's work in TV serials such like Smallville, and assumed she was an simple option for the great part of the soon-to-be loup-garou Madison in Heart. Director Kim Manners sensed Vaugier accompanied to the type a weakness like that of Lon Chaney, Jr. In The Wolf Man (1941 film)|The Wolf Man, that produced spectators understanding.Knight, pp.92–93 Conspiracy-theorist Ronald of Nightshifters was imagined by author and advising maker Ben Edlund as the affectless semi-drunk Randy Quaid as of Independence Day (1996 film)|Independence Day. However, this altered with Chris Gauthier's directing, and Edlund sensed that Ronald turned out to be a actually frosty type fans ought to appreciate.Knight, p.71 The creators contemplated Summer Glau for the part of the living dead Angela for Children Shouldn't Play with Dead Things, however she might not accept expected to arranging disputes.Knight, p.37

Charlie Harper (Two and a Half Men) - Mia

Mia (Emmanuelle Vaugier) is a dance educator, who Charlie had a crush on, and was involved to for a small when. Charlie determined not to wed Mia following she demanded that Alan and Jake should turn out of the home, solely to notice find out that Alan had wedded Kandi (Two and a Half Men)|Kandi and repositioned out. Charlie afterward grew to be sensually rash and depressed, since he absorbed that Mia was going to wed somebody other. Charlie accused Alan for destroying all things, however afterward registers that he was simply sensing for an excuse to get out of the wedding. They reunified in individual at the conclusion of season 6's Baseball Was Better With Steroids, ensuing in a cliffhanger for the season climax. In season 7's opening 818-jklpuzo, Mia shows in a lot fewer positive light. Mia queries Charlie for aid with a crooning vocation, however in actuality she shows to desire him back. By this time, Charlie had started a connection with Chelsea, and is at the moment ripped amid the 2. While in the workshop transcriptioning a demo tape, Mia queries Charlie for intercourse following disclosing

that she is a dreadful vocalist. Charlie informs Mia she can't chant, and selects Chelsea. As Charlie dashes off he revolves off Mia's mike, thus that he can't perceive her cry and swear at him. Mia was at Charlie's burial, challenging to perceive the body.

Wishmaster 3: Beyond the Gates of Hell - Cast

The principal cast of Wishmaster 3
*Jason Connery as Professor Joel Barash.
*John Novak as The Djinn
*A.J. Cook (actress)|A.J. Cook like Diana Collins
*Tobias Mehler as Greg Jansen. Later goes the service for Saint Michael the Archangel.
*Louisette Geiss as Katie York
*Aaron Smolinski as Billy Matthews
***Emmanuelle Vaugier as Elinor Smith**
*Sarah Carter as Melissa Bell
*Daniella Evangelista as Anne
*Jennifer Pudavick as Jose Rodriguez

Saw IV - Cast

*Tobin Bell as Jigsaw (Saw)|John Kramer
*Costas Mandylor as Mark Hoffman|Detective Mark Hoffman
*Scott Patterson as List of Saw characters#Peter Strahm|Agent Peter Strahm
*Betsy Russell as Jill Tuck
*Lyriq Bent as List of Saw characters#Daniel Rigg|Lieutenant Daniel Rigg
*Athena Karkanis as List of Saw characters#Lindsey Perez|Agent Lindsey Perez
*Louis Ferreira|Justin Louis as List of Saw characters#Art Blank|Art Blank
*Donnie Wahlberg as Eric Matthews (Saw)|Detective Eric Matthews
*Angus Macfadyen as List of Saw characters#Jeff Denlon|Jeff Denlon
*Dina Meyer as List of Saw characters#Allison Kerry|Detective Allison Kerry
*Marty Adams as List of Saw characters#Ivan Landsness|Ivan Landsness
*Janet Land as List of Saw characters#Rex and Morgan|Morgan
*Ron Lea as List of Saw characters#Rex and Morgan|Rex
*Sarain Boylan as List of Saw characters#Brenda|Brenda
*Billy Otis as List of Saw characters#Cecil Adams|Cecil Adams
*Kevin Rushton as List of Saw characters#Trevor|Trevor
*Simon Reynolds as Lamanna
*Mike Realba as List of Saw characters#Fisk|Detective Fisk
*Ingrid Hart as List of Saw characters#Tracy Rigg|Tracy Rigg
*James Van Patten as List of Saw characters#Trevor|Dr. Heffner

***Emmanuelle Vaugier as List of Saw characters#Addison Corday|Addison Corday**

*Noam Jenkins as List of Saw characters#Michael Marks|Michael Marks
*Tony Nappo as List of Saw characters#Gus Colyard|Gus Colyard
*Mike Butters as List of Saw characters#Paul Stallberg|Paul Stallberg
*J. Larose as List of Saw characters#Troy|Troy
*Oren Koules as List of Saw characters#Donnie Greco|Donnie Greco

Mr. Monk Gets Jury Duty - Plot synopsis

After a prolonged and hazardous pursuit via the roads of San Francisco, Leland Stottlemeyer|Captain Stottlemeyer and Randy Disher|Lieutenant Disher eventually catch Miguel Escobar (Carlos Gómez (actor)|Carlos Gómez), a dope lord whoever is the most desired individual in the United States. The capture benefits lots of public attention for Stottlemeyer and Disher. However, they are shortly ran into by FBI Special Agent Lapides (Michael Weaver), whoever has a letter for them as of the United States Attorney General. He wants them to transference Escobar over to the national political authority. Stottlemeyer is unwilling, referring to Lapides that they run to pin him on a native blood, however Lapides details out that Escobar was as well circulation narcotics in to 7 states. The national interest has been recorded, thus the federal agents must get to attempt him foremost. Stottlemeyer and Disher are to babysit Escobar till the extradition perceiving, and fall him off at the native courthouse. Elsewhere, Adrian Monk|Monk collects the information that he has been picked for jury work. Although Monk objections that he functions only, Natalie Teeger|Natalie ponders it must be high-quality for him to work as a group. After an affectless justice (Clyde Kusatsu) discharges Monk's adjuration that he could not share a bathroom with 11 additional folks, Monk discovers him self sitting in on the situation of a youthful individual designated Robert Perry, (Edo Walker) charged of knifing a individual designated Karl Pillemer (Blake Silver) in the part of the leg, and then taking the cash he is bearing. The other jurors are persuaded of the accused's culpability, and altogether ballot culpable, however Monk is the solitary holdout. He's noticed that the shot lesion and the cavity in the victim's Jeans show that Pillemer was sitting, not positioning (as he had claimed), once striked. The lesion, Monk numbers, was self-inflicted and the blade put in Perry's hand when he was sleeping thus he might pocket the cash him self. Several of the jury participants change their ballot, however Monk is preoccupied by a canine sniffing about a dumpster external the pane. Monk organizes to call to Natalie, whoever is taking him his luncheon, to call Stottlemeyer

and inform him there is a form in the dumpster. Disher discovers the body of a female with no I.D. However wearing Orthopedic footwear, and Monk recalls her as a female sitting in the gathering area once the jurors remained being picked. The ensuing day, Monk displays the jurors the towel that Pillemer applied to shoot the seeping as of his part of the leg lesion. The blood design is coherent with the towel experiencing been neatly folded, even although he asserted to have selected it up off the floor. The other jurors are persuaded, excluding for Juror No. 12, Pat (Emmanuelle Vaugier), whoever amends her ballot to culpable beforehand apathetically leaving for the amenities. Monk discovers traces of Lime on Juror No. 12's coat, simply like was applied on the dumpster to conceal the body.

Emmanuelle Vaugier - Television

Vaugier played the part of youthful, arriviste model Maria Alcobar in a 1996 chapter of Highlander: The Series. In 2004, she played Lindsey Kellogg on the brief Fox Broadcasting Company|Fox Television serials North Shore (TV series)|North Shore. She has as well had guest-star spots on Veronica Mars, Supernatural (U.S. TV series)|Supernatural, The Outer Limits (1995 TV series)|The Outer Limits, Higher Ground (TV series)|Higher Ground, Andromeda, and Charmed. She as well emerged in the Emmy Award proposed Miniseries The Beach Boys: An American Family wherever she pictured Mike Love's spouse, Suzanne. Vaugier as well finished a leading part in MOW Veiled Truth for the Lifetime Television|Lifetime Network. She is as well familiar for her part throughout the foremost 2 seasons of One Tree Hill (TV series)|One Tree Hill, as Nicki, Jake's (Bryan Greenberg) ex-girlfriend and mom to their kid, Jenny.

In 2005ndash;2006, Vaugier visitor featured in 6 chapters of CBS's hit situation comedy Two and a Half Men as Mia, a dance educator whoever Charlie Harper (Two and a Half Men)|Charlie Harper dropped in fancy with and nearly wedded. In 2005, she as well played the name type in the Painkiller Jane (film)|Painkiller Jane TV film for the Sci Fi Channel (United States)|Sci Fi Channel. However, she foremost grew to be perceived by the discipline stories group once she pictured Dr. Helen Bryce, the fancy attention of Lex Luthor (Smallville)|Lex Luthor, on the WB's hit spectacle Smallville in 2002ndash;2003.

Vaugier emerged in 2 chapters of the Fox serials Human Target (2010 TV series)|Human Target as FBI go-between Emma Barnes, whoever is foremost instituted to the show on January 26, 2010, in the chapter Embassy Row.Mitovich, Matt Webb (December 21, 2009). [http://xfinitytv.comcast.net/blogs/2009/matts-tv-news/scoop-foxs-human-target-sets-sights-on-vaugier/ Scoop! Fox's Human Target Sets

Sights on Vaugier]. Xfinity|XfinityTV. Retrieved July 4, 2011.

Vaugier at the moment has a repeating part on the Syfy serials Lost Girl (TV series)|Lost Girl as The Morrigan, the guider of the Dark Fae.Gamei, Tariq (December 29, 2011). [http://www.spoilertv.com/2011/12/lost-girl-emmanuelle-vaugier-returning.html Lost Girl – Emmanuelle Vaugier restoring for dim Fae arch at the conclusion of season 2]. Spoiler TV. Retrieved June 30, 2012.

The Other Side (The Outer Limits) - Cast

* Ralph Macchio as Dr. Neal Eberhardt
* Susanna Hoffman as Janice Claymore
* Michael Sarrazin as Marty Kilgore
* Scott Swanson as Emil Dobkins
* Aaron Smolinski as Adam
* **Emmanuelle Vaugier as Lisa Dobkins**
* Trevor White (actor)|Trevor White as Vince Carter
* P. Lynn Johnson as Vera Dobkins

Unearthed (film)

'Unearthed' is a 2006 in film|2006 terror feature, directed by Matthew Leutwyler (Dead Breakfast) and leading Emmanuelle Vaugier (Saw II) and Luke Goss. This giant film unlocked on November 9, 2007 as one of the 8 Films to Die For in the After Dark Films Horrorfest.

Painkiller Jane (film)

'Painkiller Jane' is a made-for-television film founded on the Painkiller Jane|comic publication type of the similar designation. It was foremost transmit on the Sci Fi Channel (United States)|Sci-Fi Channel within December 2005. The 2-hour feature stars Emmanuelle Vaugier as the nominal heroine. The feature varies notably as of the tale of the funny publication type.

The film was a backdoor pilot for a feasible TV serials, that was finally accepted. The Painkiller Jane (TV series)|Painkiller Jane TV serials shows to be a Reboot (continuity)|reboot of the TV-movie, abandoning the film's backstory and beginning afresh.

Mirrors 2 - Cast

* Nick Stahl as Max Matheson
  *** Emmanuelle Vaugier as Elizabeth Reigns**
* Christy Carlson Romano|Christy Romano as Jenna McCarty
* Evan Jones (actor)|Evan Jones as Henry Schow
* William Katt as Jack Matheson
* Lawrence Turner as Keller Landreaux
* Stephanie Honoré|Stephanie Honoré Sanchez as Eleanor Reigns
* Jon Michael Davis as Ryan Parker
* Lance E. Nichols as Detective Huston
* Wayne Pére as Detective Piccirilli
* Jenny Shakeshaft as Kayla
* Ann Mckenzie as Doctor Beaumont

Far Cry (film) - Cast

* Til Schweiger as Jack Carver
  *** Emmanuelle Vaugier as Valerie Constatine**
* Natalia Avelon as Katja Chernov
* Michael Paré as Paul Summers
* Clint Howard as Lead Scientist (uncredited)
* Craig Fairbrass as Mike
* Udo Kier as Dr. Krieger
* Mike Dopud as S Sgt. Ryder
* Chris Coppola as Emilio
* Ralf Möller as Max Cardinal
* Don S. Davis as General Roderick
* Michael Eklund
* Jay Brazeau as Ralph
* Michael Rogers (actor)|Michael Rogers as Mercenary Kelly
* Anthony Bourdain as Scientist (Tad Chanko)

Emmanuelle Vaugier

'Emmanuelle Vaugier' (born June 23, 1976) is a Canadians|Canadian feature female actor, vocalist, model, and TV female actor whoever

has had repeating parts as Minor types in CSI: NY#Jessica Angell|Detective Jessica Angell on CSI: NY, List of Two and a Half Men characters#Recurring|Mia on Two and a Half Men, Characters of Smallville#Dr. Helen Bryce|Dr. Helen Bryce on Smallville, Human Target (2010 TV series)#Recurring characters|FBI Special Agent Emma Barnes on Human Target (2010 TV series)|Human Target, and like The Morrigan on Lost Girl (TV series)|Lost Girl. In characteristic features, Vaugier has emerged next to Michael Caine and Robert Duvall in Secondhand Lions. She emerged as List of Saw characters#Addison Corday|Addison Corday in Saw II and Saw IV, and she had a helping part in the Josh Hartnett feature 40 Days and 40 Nights.

Painkiller Jane (film) - Cast

Emmanuelle Vaugier as Capt. Jane Elizabeth Browning/Painkiller Jane - The show's protagonist

*Eric Dane as Nick Pierce
*Richard Roundtree as Colonel Ian Watts - Jane's supervising officer
*Nels Lennarson as Agent Thorpe
*Richard Harmon as Squeak
*Tate Donovan as Dr. Graham Knight/Lucas Insley
*Venus Terzo as Carla Browning - Jane's female sibling

Secondhand Lions - Plot

In 1962 in the Texas boondocks, 14-year aged Walter Caldwell (Haley Joel Osment) is left by his reckless, crooked mom, Mae (Kyra Sedgwick), to live for the summertime with his reclusive, bachelor great-uncles, Hub (Robert Duvall) and Garth (Michael Caine) McCann, bros indicated to have a confidential prosperity In the out of the ordinary characteristic Secondhand Lions: One Screenplay's Wild Ride in Hollywood on the film DVD, the creators address about in what way strange it ought to have been for Tommy Lee Jones, whoever is 6 annums junior compared to Robert Duvall, to play Hub, the aged male sibling, when Duval was suggested for Garth, the junior male sibling. At the time of shooting, Duvall was 72 and Michael Caine was 70. On the letter as of Mae, the annum is 1962. If Hub and Garth remained the similar ages as Duvall and Caine in 1962, that ought to create them 24 and 22, correspondingly, in 1914 once World War I started.

. Walter is specified a area in the loft wherever he discovers a picture of a attractive female, whoever he afterward absorbs is Jasmine (Emmanuelle Vaugier), Hub's one genuine fancy. Soon following, relatives Ralph and Helen turn up with their kids, anticipating for a probability at the prosperity. Thinking Walter is as well following it,

they intimidate nurture heed, creating him run. Walter produces his course to a gas facility, and utilizes a telephone kiosk to call the Court reporter|court informing educational institution that his mom informed him she was visiting solely to absorb she is not there. The 2 uncles perceive him; Hub is pleased to perceive him on his course, however Garth persuades Hub to carry him back home.

Walter starts resolving in, transacting with his uncles' strange customs, such like Hub's sleepwalking at nighttime in that he relives aged brawls, as well like their everyday procedure of shooting at journeying clerk for glee. Curious, Walter proposes they at minimum perceive a pitch; they finish end up purchasing a clay chump Launcher. Hub commands a lion as of a cirque creature merchant, intending to stage its head following slaying it; nevertheless, they finish end up with an growing older, docile Lioness. Walter designations her Jasmine, infuriating Hub. Later, Hub progresses out loading 50 pound bags of Purina Lion Chow, arriving him in the infirmary. He shortly recovers and is hungry; the 3 additionally luncheon at a way aspect store. Four Greaser (subculture)|Greasers admit, annoying Hub whoever effortlessly defeats them in a brawl. In their nonappearance, Ralph and Helen's boys coincidentally discharge Jasmine as of her clunker simply like Hub, Garth and Walter return. Walter looks for Jasmine, and discovers her in the Cornfield, that goes her spic-and-span wilderness home. When Walter notes Hub lecturing the 4 toughs, Garth clarifies it's Hub's out of the ordinary talk for what a young man demand to comprehend. Since the Lioness must hold Ralph and Helen off, Hub and Garth choose to let Walter hold Jasmine as a pet.

Garth as well clarifies their bygones via the tale. On the crepuscule of World War I, Hub and Garth came in France simply like Germany occupied the region. They shortly noticed themself shanghaiing|shanghaied and enlisted in to the French Foreign Legion|Legion, that guided them to brawl in numerous fights. After the conflict, Garth grew to be a guide in Africa, when Hub journeyed the planet. During his journeys, Hub encountered and dropped in fancy with Jasmine, a goddess guaranteed to a strong Sheikh|Sheik. When Hub saved her, the Sheik set a cost of 10,000 gold coin|gold fragments on Hub's head, holding them in invariable hazard as of assassins and reward huntsmen. Finally, Hub organized for Garth, in the semblance of a reward huntsman, to get him close to the Sheik, when Garth composed the recompense. Hub additionally struggled and gained a fight opposed to the Sheik however spared his existence. He cautioned the Sheik if this Vendetta did not finish, his existence would; this stops the Sheik's manhunt. When Walter queries to perceive further, Garth speaks he should notice find out the rest as of Hub.

Later, Walter wakes up Hub as of a attack of sleepwalking to inquire about Jasmine's destiny. Hub divulges Jasmine and their unborn kid passed away in labor. Knowing no different existence, Hub restored to the Legion to get away his affliction, till he withdrew with Garth to their Texas ranch. Walter additionally registers Garth's narratives could be genuine, however queries Hub to assert it, eversince his mom on every relevant occasion informs reposes. Hub replies with a bit of his What Every Boy Needs to Know... Talk, that the real veracity is not like essential as the faith in dreams like high-quality conquering over bad, merit, and genuine fancy. Seeing in what way a lot Hub fails his Jasmine, Walter queries Hub to pledge to be about to offer him the rest of the talk once he's aged enough; Hub grudgingly concurs. As a effect, Walter and his uncles shape an even closer bond. Late one night, Walter wakes up to perceive Garth strolling out to the shed and privately tails him, trailing him to a area beneath the shed, that is packed with cash.

On one other nighttime, Walter's mom and her present gallant, a assumed undisclosed inspector designated Stan, turn up. While the uncles slumber, Stan and Mae request that Walter disclose the place of the prosperity, asserting Hub and Garth remained really Bank robbery|bank thiefs, that Jasmine was their partner in crime, and the cash is theirs for the seizing. To Mae's disappointment, Walter selects to trust in his uncles in lieu of her. Angered, Stan hauls Walter to the shed, disclosing he's in profound arrearage. Walter additionally informs Stan to protect him self beforehand kicking him amid the legs. Walter runs to the home, bygones the Cornfield, wherever Stan thumps him down and starts striking him. Sensing Walter in hazard, the Lioness appears as of the Cornfield to assault Stan, leaving him poorly mauled. Awakened by the ruckus, Hub and Garth notice the aged Lioness passed away of heart letdown. Hub and Garth clarify Jasmine was safeguarding her abecedarian, and Walter with pride notices she was a actual lion... At the conclusion.

The following day, Walter departs with his mom, whoever is forced by the uncles to get free of Stan. She answers she plans to fall him off in Las Vegas Valley|Vegas. However, at one point on the way, Mae clarifies Stan must be remaining with them to recuperate. Sick of Mae, Walter queries her to eventually do somewhat that is finest for myself for at one point. Soon, Hub and Garth are considerably happy to perceive Walter's return. However, the young man maintains there have to be changes: his uncles must have to be included in items like Little League and Parent-Teacher Association|PTA gatherings, and to halt undertaking hazardous feats, as he desires them to perish of aged age.

17 annums afterward, an grown-up Walter (Josh Lucas), has come to be the animation drawer of the funny strip Walter and Jasmine, founded on his encounters with his uncles, at the moment either 90 annums of age. He is forewarned by the Sheriff of his uncles' demises as of a disappointed flying stunt with their biplane. Their must declares The child receives it altogether. Just plant us in the darn yard, following to the silly lion. A chopper bearing the emblem Sahara Petroleum additionally moves down nearby the Homestead, and a individual (Eric Balfour) treads out with his youthful boy (Daniel Brooks). Approaching Walter, he clarifies when stopping by

closeby for a trade journey, he perceived regarding Hub and Garth's demises on the information and acknowledged the designations as the 2 Americans in narratives informed to him as a youthful young man by his granddad, a real rich Sheik. He named them 'my nearly all respected adversaries. The solely males whoever at any time outsmarted myself.' When the man's youthful boy (Daniel Brooks) queries Walter if his uncles remained certainly actual, that they actually existed, Walter affirms, Yeah. They actually existed.

Lost Girl (TV series) - Recurring cast

*** Emmanuelle Vaugier as Evony Fleurette Marquise: The Morrígan. The merciless, beguiling, and vindictive guider of the native Dark Fae, she may thaw and dematerialize flesh with her handle. She is a leanan Sidhe and runs a aptitude organization in the mortal society, wherever she appears for youthful performers and creators when taking their lives in interchange for celebrity. (Original Pilot; Season One, Two, Three, Four)**

* Paul Amos as Vex: a Mesmer. A sadomasochist Dark Fae with a sardonic and bawdy feel of comedy, he may command people's principals opposed to their must, containing making them to eliminate themself either effect kill. Vex is a best-loved of the Dark Elders and has a like-hate connection with The Morrígan, servicing like her hit individual. He plays a crucial part opposed to the Garuda once Bo abecedarian him for her group and he utilizes his authorities to detain the Garuda utilizing Trick's blood to inverse the Blood Laws and reignite a conflict amid Light and Dark. (Original Pilot; Season One, Two, Three, Four)

* Inga Cadranel as Aife (Pseudonym|aka Saskia in Season One): a Succubus and Bo's birthing mom. She is the girl of Trick, the Blood King, and Isabeau. After rebelling opposed to the Truce forced amid the Light and Dark Fae and slaying a Dark Elder, she is provided to the Dark Fae for implementation. Instead of being set to demise, she endures numerous centuries of internment, abuse, and assault by a Dark King beforehand she is capable to get away. She masterminds a self-murder bombarding that executes nearly all of the Light Fae Elders and seriously injures The Ash. (Season One, Three, Four)

* Rachel Skarsten as Tamsin: a Valkyrie. Dyson's spic-and-span investigator collaborator following Hale grew to be the performing Ash. A soldier of fortune and reward huntsman functioning for the Dark Fae, she is not happy with being enforced to work with a Light Fae collaborator. She is constructing a instance opposed to Bo for assaulting and feeding on a associate of the Dark Fae, and renditioning him knocked out. Initially, she has no difficulty displaying her aversion for Bo either Dyson's mash with her, however progresses an attraction and regard for Bo, to the

point of interrogating her own loyalties. (Season Three, Four)

* Tim Rozon as Massimo: The Druid. (Season Three, Four)

* Kate Trotter as The The Norns|Norn: an Ancient with the power to allow one selves sturdiest wish in interchange for that that they contain big-ticket. When Bo was battling her mom, Aife, Dyson pursued her interference, for the second time in his existence, and presented her his wolf in restore for conveying his potency to Bo; however he did not understand that what he at the moment cherished nearly all was his fancy for Bo, and The Norn took his capacity to fancy her either anybody other, in lieu. (In List of Lost Girl episodes#ep59|End of a Line the Voodoo enchantress Laveau informed Dyson that his fancy jail – I.e. His fancy for Bo – was of his personal creating.) The Norn restored Dyson's fancy zeal following Kenzi endangered to cut down her Sacred Tree with a chainsaw. (Season One, Two)

* Rob Archer as Bruce: a guard and Hatchet individual for The Morrígan (species unknown). (Season Three, Four)

* Clé Bennett as the Ash: guider of the Light Fae. He desires Bo to pick orientation with the Light, and commands Lauren to notice a means to divert Bo thus like to stop her as of assaulting and slaying Vex – that might have jeopardized the tranquility amid the Fae Clans and specified the Morrígan a cause to finish Bo. He is poorly hurt in an murder aim by Bo's mom, Aife, and left in a unconscious state on existence aid at the conclusion of Season One. (Original Pilot; Season One)

* Vincent Walsh as Lachlan: the Ash. He gains the placing of The Ash within a bawdy chase following the foregoing Ash is left unconscious. He is a stickler for commands and a controlling guider whoever does not dither to declare his power, castigate disobedience, and undertake off with anybody whoever intimidates the Light Fae and the confidential being of the Fae. He is disclosed to be a Nāga, experiencing violently missed his different crowns for their bane. The Nāga has the power to eliminate the Garuda with its venom; however with the mislaying of his different crowns, Lachlan understands he can't conquer his very old adversary and beforehand positioned so as to face him in a brawl to the demise he has Lauren draw his bane thus that she may spin it in to a armament for Bo to eliminate the Garuda with. (Season Two)

* Lina Roessler as Ciara: familiar like a Fairy Queen. The fighter girl of a Fairy and Scáthach with authorities of lightning-fast speed, she educated the handcraft of conflict to Dyson and his wolf-shapeshifter package. She is a bygones fancy of Dyson, and they are reunified following the transition of centuries and come to be starry-eyed involved; however though she is in fancy with Dyson, he is incapable to answer in sort eversince The Norn has taken his capacity to fancy. While she is

originally handled frostily by Bo and Kenzi, Bo finally appears to review her a pal. She is slayed by the Garuda once she moves in fore of Bo to safeguard her as of the push of his sword. (Season Two)

* Anthony Lemke as Ryan Lambert: a Dark Fae Loki. He is a rich socialite whoever gathered a prosperity as an creator, Alchemist, and provider of scarce and expensive articles. He impacts Bo's anniversary party to offer her an etched bangle that, she afterward absorbs, may safeguard her as of a types of Fae. Without her realizing that he is Dark, the 2 come to be concupiscent sweethearts following Bo's connection with Dyson stops, and her amorousness with Lauren is disturbed once Nadia is disseminated as of her state of unconsciousness. (Season Two)

* Hayley Nault as the Nain Rouge: a heavenly Fae will that likes to notice deplorable happenings and materializes as a youthful female child. The Nain Rouge shows to Bo once inexplicable Fae demises start to happen and presents Bo a apparition in which she is the principle of Trick's demise. When the reemergence of the Fae's very old adversary, the Garuda, starts to produce odd happenings in essence, the Nain Rouge replies Bo's call to display herself and informs Bo that for her to conquer the Garuda she wants to construct a unified group of Light and Dark Fae. (Season Two)

* Raoul Trujillo as The Garuda: an very old and fiendish strong adversary of the Fae. The Garuda transforms in to a huge burning eagle, and may own and command its sufferers. Its origin of nourishment is rage and fury, and may solely be slayed with the bane of a Nāga. When the Blood King (Trick) records the Truce and Blood Laws that finished the Great War amid Light and Dark, the Garudas abate as they starve to demise till solely one is left, still existing inactive for eons. When Trick utilizes his blood authorities to halt Aife as of damaging and slaying Bo, it resuscitates the Garuda, that additionally appears in seek of Trick to influence him in to utilizing his blood to revoke the Laws and reignite the conflict amid Light and Dark. He is slayed by Bo with Lachlan's bane. (Season Two)

* Shawn Doyle as Dr. Isaac Taft: a insane mortal scientist and Fae huntsman. He shows at Lauren's flat providing a study prize following she nose-dives to be at the out of the ordinary presentment pomp. Dr. Taft Deceptively benches Lauren till, following some disappointed tries, he persuaded her to unite him in carrying out cutting edge health study in his undisclosed research lab. He understands regarding the Fae and Lauren's participation with the mystic race, and desires her know-how about them to inflict atrocious vengeance opposed to the Fae following his male sibling was beheaded by one and he was accused for the felony. Taft kidnapps Dyson to withdraw his DNA for employ on him self, however Lauren privately sabotages the DNA transplantation and revolves him in to a human-Cabbit cross. He is slayed and consume by Dyson. (Season Three)

* Deborah Odell as Stella Nashira: a Lodestar. She is enlisted by Trick to adviser Bo in her readying for the quizzes she has to face throughout The Dawning. She and Trick fall In fancy and leave alltogether for Scotland in the season climax. (Season Three)

* Christine Horne as The Keeper: the interrogator of The Una Mens. (Season Four)

* Athena Karkanis as Nadia: Lauren's mortal sweetheart. She escorted Lauren to the Congo as a shutterbug and when there The Ash triggered her to be stricken by a strange sickness that departs her in a state of unconsciousness – thus manipulating Lauren in to pledged bondage to him and the Light Fae. Bo is enforced to eliminate her once she goes controlled by the Garuda and charges Lauren, alarming her existence. (Season Two)

* Aaron Ashmore as Nate: Kenzi's lover. Kenzi and Nate applied to be neighbours once she was 6 annums aged and they encounter once more by coexistence sixteen annums afterward once he replies an advertisement for a performer gig at Bo's shock anniversary party. Kenzi breaks breaks up with him once the Garuda's menace is nearly all impending and might have imperiled his existence. (Season Two)

* Kyle Schmid as Rainer: a renegade Fae. (Season Four)

* Ali Liebert as Crystal: a server at the beanery Lauren operated in when in hiding. (Season Four)

* Mia Kirshner as Clio: an Elemental Nymph. (Season Four)

Blonde and Blonder - Plot

Two stupid Blondes, Dee Twiddle (Pamela Anderson) and Dawn St. Dom (Denise Richards), encounter every one other at their foremost lecture within flying educational institution. Dee is a big-breasted non-amateur danseur with a pet turtle, Virgil, whoever has a gas difficulty. Dawn is a erstwhile assistant whoever has attempted to be a danseur. After gathering with every one other in flying educational institution, they get off in their plane short of the teacher. When they notice that it's their foremost lecture, the Blondes alarm and smash in to a golf program. The Blondes endure the smash with no wounds. The Blondes finally come to be acquaintances and they notice that they have been neighbors for almost a annum.

Dee chooses to aid Dawn get a swaying gig at the Beaver Patch Lounge. Meanwhile, the Vancouver Italian Mafia chooses to assay Lou Rimoli, a

erstwhile cabal associate and present informer, whoever is operating the Beaver Patch Lounge. Rimoli is being saved by 2 representatives. The Godfather of the crowd directs 2 feminine assassins, Cat (Emmanuelle Vaugier) and Kit (Meghan Ory) to assay Rimoli. The assassins ensue. However, Rimoli is killed right beforehand Dee and Dawn's tryout. The Mobsters, Leo (Kevin Farley) and Swan (John P. Farley|John Farley) remained assumed to screen what was occurring, following identifying Dee and Dawn run as of the association, they error the Blondes for being the notorious assassins Cat and Kit.

Believing that Dee and Dawn are assassins, Leo and Swan proffer them $250,000 to take out Hang Wong (Byron Mann), the head of the Triads in Niagara Falls, Ontario. Dee and Dawn concur, however they consider that they have to take Wong on a date. Federal representatives find the design to eliminate Wong and come after the fair Duo as well considering they are Cat and Kit. The Godfather directs Leo and Swan to come after the young ladies to create certain Wong receives Whacked. Once the fair Duo turn up in Niagara Falls, they resolve at a gambling establishment guesthouse and refuge, that Mr. Wong possesses. Cat and Kit as well turn up there and notice find out that Dee and Dawn are professing to be them and have been the employed assassins. They design to get vengeance since Dee and Dawn took their standing for whacking Rimoli and are professing to be them to eliminate Wong.

While Dawn is conquering cash at the gambling establishment, Dee encounters Mr. Wong throughout his gathering with Leo and Swan. Dee informs Wong that Leo and Swan employed her to display him a high-quality time. Federal representatives mark Dee with Wong in the gambling establishment, and pursuit them. Wong chooses to kidnap Dee and bears her to his sailboat. Meanwhile, they are pursued by the national representatives, Dawn (Denise Richards|Richards), Cat and Kit. The national representatives and police force get everybody in to care.

Back at the gambling establishment, the police force capture Kit and Cat, and as well Wong for abducting Dee. Dawn eventually discovers her dream man and with the millions of bucks Dawn gained at the gambling establishment, Dee and Dawn demonstrate Dee and Dawn's Famous Turtle Sanctuary in the boondocks wherever they solely have one turtle however pledge to have further shortly.

List of Two and a Half Men characters - Mia

Mia (Emmanuelle Vaugier, season 3 repeating, seasons 5–7, 9 guest), a dance educator who Charlie Harper dropped in fancy with throughout the Two and a Half Men (season 3)|third season. She received him to spotless up his play by not consuming nor smoking like a lot, not

wearing bowling shirts as well like not consuming flesh. However, he breaks breaks up with her following he goes fed up with the way she was attempting to command his conduct. She additionally bears a assignment in New York. She returns in the direction of the conclusion of the 3rd season once her swaying cluster appears to municipality, and she queries Charlie for his sperm thus she may have a darling. He tries however nose-dives, and he additionally propositions wedding to her, in that she receives. Initially, Alan was their marriage organizer, nevertheless following a great affair with Mia's father and mother, they concur to proceed to Las Vegas and elope. Just like they are about to be wedded, Mia insinuates that Alan and Jake must be moving out following they wed, and Charlie declines to hurl out his kin. They split off the commitment and she departs. Mia returns in the 5th season once Charlie perceives that she is wedding one other individual, and he tries to gain her back, however her dad hits him out. She returns once more the 6th and 7th seasons following her annulment in desires that Charlie must aid her with a new-found crooning vocation. She's a alarming vocalist. Charlie additionally has to pick amid Mia and his then-fiancee Chelsea. After a lot thought, Charlie selects Chelsea and renounces Mia at the transcriptioning workshop. Mia as well produces a brief visitor emergence in the 9th season opening at Charlie's burial.

Blonde and Blonder - Cast

* Pamela Anderson as Dee Twiddle
* Denise Richards as Dawn St. Dom
* **Emmanuelle Vaugier as Cat**
* Meghan Ory as Kit, Cats Assistant
* Kevin Farley as Leo, a Gangster
* John P. Farley|John Farley as Swan, a Gangster
* Joey Aresco as Agent Campbell
* Garry Chalk as Agent Gardenia
* Byron Mann as Mr. Wong
* Jay Brazeau as Louie Ramoli
* Woody Jeffreys as Ken, Dawns Dreamguy
* John P. Farley|John Farley as Leutant Porter
* John Tench as Evangelos, Ramolies Partner
* Alex Bruhanski as Gangsterboss Godfather
* Phoenix Ly as One Eye, one of Wangs Killers
* Kyle Labine as the new Bellboy

Episodes of Highlander (season 4) - Supporting cast

* Soumaya Akaaboune ... Aliya
* Philip Akin ... Charlie DeSalvo
* Sean Allan ... Simon Killian
* Guy Amram ... Kelly
* Eileen Barrett ... Alice Markum
* Veronique Baylaucq ... Annie
* Kabir Bedi ... Kamir
* Luc Bernard ... Inspector Deon
* Wolfgang Bodison ... Andrew Cord
* Crispin Bonham-Carter ... Danny Cimoli
* Stéphane Boucher ... Edward Bellamy
* Geoffroy Boutan ... Claude Massanet
* Benjamin Boyer ... David Shapiro
* Chris Bradford ... Joe Dawson (Highlander)|Young Joe Dawson
* Jeremy Brudenell ... Robert de Valicourt
* Patrick Burgel ... Albert
* Lisa Butler ... Melissa
* Nadia Cameron ... Rebecca Horne
* Nicholas Campbell ... Kit O'Brady
* Sean Campbell ... Sergeant Merion
* Valeria Cavalli ... Dominique
* Nicola Cavendish ... Queen Anne
* Carl Chase ... Robert Davis / 2 episodes
* Byron Chief-Moon ... James Coltec
* Rae Dawn Chong ... Claudia Jardine
* Garrison Chrisjohn ... Dr. Weldon
* Ewan Sudsy Clark ... George Lalonde
* Morgan Cooke ... Antoine
* Luc Corbeil ... Merriman
* Garvin Cross ... Ray
* Roger Daltrey ... Hugh Fitzcairn
* Stephen Dimopoulos ... Vince Petrovic
* Tim Dixon ... Harry
* Vernon Dobtcheff ... Hamad
* Yan Epstein ... Jean Dumar
* Ben Feitelson ... Nasir Al Deneb
* Michel Feller ... Mikel
* Myles Ferguson ... Kenny
* Brent Fidler ... Jeremy Beaufort
* Shannon Finnegan ... Sarah
* Roland Gift ... Xavier St. Cloud
* Elizabeth Gracen ... Amanda (Highlander)|Amanda / 5 episodes

* Manuel Guillot ... Emile
* Anna Hagan ... Mary MacLeod
* Ron Halder ... Walter Graham
* Jamie Harris (actor)|Jamie Harris ... Daniel Geiger
* Phil Hayes (actor)|Phil Hayes ... Alan Wells
* Rachel Hayward ... Valerie Meech
* Ocean Hellman ... Alexa Bond
* Fred Henderson ... Desantis
* Tim Henry ... Jim Rainey
* Anna Hogan ... Mary MacLeod
* Laurie Holden ... Debra Campbell
* Lisa Howard ... Anne Lindsey / 2 episodes
* Peter Hudson ... James Horton (Highlander)|James Horton
* Anthony Hyde ... Nathan Stern
* Robert Iseman ... Mike
* Michael J. Jackson (actor)|Michael J. Jackson ... Sean Burns / 2 chapters
* Liliana Komorowska ... Mara Leonin
* Simon Kunz ... Damon Case
* Darcy Laurie ... Harry Kant
* Kevin Lesmister ... Earl of Welsley
* Justin Louis ... Peter Kanis
* Roger Lumont ... Marco Mastina
* David Mackay ... Gremio
* Laura Marine ... Nancy Goddard
* Sue Mathew ... Vashti
* Scott McNeil ... Robert MacLeod
* Kevin McNulty (actor)|Kevin McNulty ... David Markum
* Graham McTavish ... Charlie
* Travis MacDonald ... Mark Roszca
* Andrew MacGregor ... Donal
* Patrick Mille ... Jean Philippe de LeFaye III
* Kristin Minter ... Rachel MacLeod / 3 episodes
* Billy J. Mitchell ... Brian McSwain
* Alison Moir ... Diane Terrin
* Robert Moloney ... Kevin McSwain
* Romina Mondello ... Irina Galati
* Gresby Nash ... Andrew Donnelly
* Carsten Norgaard ... Kanwulf
* Tracy Olson ... Lord Sewell
* Peter Outerbridge ... Paul Kinman
* Cécile Pallas ... Gina de Valicourt
* Molly Parker ... Alice Ramsey
* Gerard Plunkett ... James Bailey

* Michael Preston ... Terence Kincaid
* Benjamin Ratner ... Bryce Korland
* Jeffrey Renn ... Young Ian Bancroft
* Callum Keith Rennie ... Tyler King
* Kim Restell ... Julie
* Christine Rivere ... Nadia
* Struan Rodger ... Bonnie Prince Charlie
* Greg Rogers ... Detective Sheridan
* Ricco Ross ... Kassim
* Jenafor Ryane ... Alicia
* Karim Salah ... Boadin Al Deneb
* George Salmon ... James
* William Samples ... Bruce
* Tony Scanling ... Lord Keating
* Dougray Scott ... Warren Cochrane
* Tomer Sisley ... Reza
* Veena Sood ... Shandra Devane / 2 episodes
* Brent Stait ... Colonel Ramsey
* Jill Teed ... Kaayla Brooks
* Carla Temple ... Denise
* Venus Terzo ... The Duchess
* John Tierney ... Angus
* Stacey Travis ... Agent Delaney
* Stephen Tremblay ... Jacob Galati / 2 episodes
* Yee Jee Tso ... Gerald
* Ann Turkel ... Kristin
* Christine Upright-Letain ... Andrea Henson
* **Emmanuelle Vaugier ... Maria Alcobar**
* Pruitt Taylor Vince ... Mikey Bellows
* Louise Vincent ... Lina Cimoli
* Matthew Walker (actor)|Matthew Walker ... Ian MacLeod
* Jesse Joe Walsh ... Jack Shapiro / 2 episodes
* Dave 'Squatch' Ward ... Cisco
* Marc Warren ... Morgan d'Estaing
* Alec Willows ... Martin Millay
* Peter Wingfield ... Methos / 8 episodes
* Joel Wirkkunen ... McPhee

It's Christmas, Carol!

'It's Christmas, Carol!', an alteration of Charles Dickens' A Christmas

Carol, debuted on the Hallmark Channel onto November 18, 2012. It tails Carol (Emmanuelle Vaugier), a sour workhorse, that receives a rouse up call as of her dead employer, Eve (Carrie Fisher). Eve shows like the 3 dissimilar specters of Christmas (Past, Present, Future). In the conclusion, Carol registers what she'd missed over the annums and amends her methods.

Dolan's Cadillac (film) - Plot

Middle educational institution past educator Tom Robinson (Wes Bentley) lives in Las Vegas Valley|Las Vegas with cherished spouse Elizabeth (Emmanuelle Vaugier). On a equine riding journey out in the barren one day, Elizabeth appears athwart a mortal circulation transact moved poor, with mobster Jimmy Dolan (Christian Slater) carrying out a individual. Elizabeth is noticed, nevertheless, and scarcely flees Dolan's thugs firing at her. She releases her telephone, that the thugs notice and employ to recognize her. Soon following Elizabeth discovers in her home a scary dispatch (in the shape of a dead body with darn lips) disclosing her to hold still.

The Robinsons proceed to the powers, and an formal (Al Sapienza) confesses them in to the Witness Protection programme. Not prolonged afterward, Elizabeth wakens up abruptly throughout the nighttime as she wants to barf, that she bears as a mark that she is expectant. Believing her dream has come genuine, she receives enthused and dashes out of their guesthouse to purchase gestation quizzes, Tom ensuing following her. When she attempts to commence their automobile, it blows up in fore of Tom, slaying Elizabeth.

Devastated, Tom starts consuming, and finally chooses to pursue vengeance opposed to Dolan. He acquisitions a handgun, a huge Smith Wesson Model 500, and tails Dolan about municipality, finally going following him one nighttime. But beforehand he may take the shot, a competitor trade of Dolan's jerks a drive-by, that nosedives since Dolan's Cadillac is disclosed to be impregnable.

Robinson resumes to come after Dolan, whoever shortly notes and absorbs his ID. The 2 encounter at a Rest Stop in the Nevada barren, finishing with a conflict in that Dolan permits Robinson to live (albeit all in up), trusting existence to be further irritating for Robinson compared to demise.

Undeterred, Robinson receives a assignment with a building team functioning on the ways Dolan frequently journeys. After strenuous readying, Robinson places his trap: a colossus chuckhole profound in the way, great sufficient to setup a automobile however not thus great as to permit Dolan to get away by beginning the entrances. When Dolan's automobile drops in to the cavity, the driver is slayed and one other traveler (Greg Bryk) is hurt. Dolan shoots him as a compassion slaying and out of irritation, as either his legs remained broken and he always screamed in pain.

Once Dolan has been confined, Robinson produces his existence familiar, disclosing Dolan that he is a automobilist whoever observed what had occured. Dolan, nevertheless, finally registers that the automobilist is, in reality, Robinson, and starts to implore Robinson to let him proceed. Robinson starts to fill up the vessel entombed alive|hole with grime, ongoing to insult Dolan with chances of his get away, not one of that come to completion.

The formal as of the Witness Protection programme shortly calls Robinson to inform him that Dolan had been on his course to a chief undertaking including kid intercourse circulation, a felony that ought to have demolished Dolan. Robinson does not heed, nevertheless, and finishes stuffing the cavity up. Robinson lays solid blocks over the Cadillac, when Dolan shrieks as of inside the cavity.

The formal calls back and informs Robinson they at the moment have sufficient for a condemnation. Robinson releases the telephone and laughs maniacally.

Mindstorm (film) - Cast

Source:

***Emmanuelle Vaugier - Tracey Wellman**
*Eric Roberts - David Mendez
*Michael Ironside - Senator William Armitage
*Antonio Sabato Jr. - FBI Agent Dan Oliver
*William B. Davis - Doctor Parish
*Clarence Williams III - Walter Golden

Unearthed (film) - Cast

Emmanuelle Vaugier as 'Sheriff Annie Flynn'
*Luke Goss as 'Kale'
*Beau Garrett as 'Caya'
*Charles Q. Murphy as 'Hank'
*Tonantzin Carmelo as 'Nodin'
*Whitney Able as 'Ally'
*Tommy Dewey as 'Charlie'

*M.C. Gainey as 'Rob Horn'
*Russell Means as 'Grandpa'
*Miranda Bailey as 'Carla'
*Ric Barbera as 'Curtis'
*Chris Andrew Ciulla as 'Kelly'
*Jason Hamer as 'Jason'
*Jim Jepson as 'Ranch Hand'
*Mark Kelly (actor)|Mark Kelly as 'Frank ~ Trucker'
*Deborah Offner as 'Yanya ~ Waitress'

The Other Side (The Outer Limits) - Plot

Dr. Neal Eberhardt (Ralph Macchio), a erstwhile young man mastermind moved agonizingly to germ, researches brain-damaged and unconscious cases anticipating to absorb in what way the cerebrum reroutes its normal self. Despite experiencing a insurgent spic-and-span engine to work with - the Neural Intercortex Stimulation Array either NISA - Dr. Eberhardt is acquiring not anywhere. To create interests falling short of a standard, his cherished helper Vince Carter has simply exit. But abruptly, Neal has a success. The cerebrum ripples of 2 unconscious cases, Adam (Aaron Smolinski) and Lisa (Emmanuelle Vaugier), fall in to synchronize when they are hooked up to the NISA and one of them murmurs the other's designation. Neal understands he's on to somewhat and informs his employer, Marty Kilgore (Michael Sarrazin). What Neal does not comprehend is that Adam and Lisa have landed in an idyllic collateral awareness and are dropping in fancy. As Adam and Lisa get to comprehend every one other, Neal resumes his study, joined at the moment by his ex-girlfriend and coworker Janice Claymore (Susannah Hoffman). Desperate to attempt the method on different unconscious topics, Neal misses forbearance and produces the trip him self. After assigning him self a measured overdose of Phenobarbital, he hooks him self up to NISA and starts him self in to Adam and Lisa's society. He latches a cast, however he's tugged back at the final minute, leaving him further intended compared to at any time to notice a means to save his cases as of the other aspect. But undertake they actually desire to be saved? Or is it actually Neal that desires to cross over to the other aspect?

My 5 Wives - Plot

A rich Los Angeles terra firma creator, Monte Peterson, journeys to Utah anticipating to open a ski refuge following his 3rd wedding stops in annulment. He competes opposed to an bad banker, Preston Gates, anticipating to grab terra firma as of the defaulting agriculturists to obtain command for crowd financiers whoever desire to construct a gambling establishment.

After conquering a terra firma auction sale, Monte's pal clarifies the polygamous historical conventions of the zone. Monte should unite the kirk to acquisition the terra firma. He absorbs the assets he has purchased contains the erstwhile owner's wives, that upsets Monte considerably till he receives a look at the females (Judy Tylor, Kate Luyben, Angelika Baran).

Monte weds altogether 3 and is enthused till he uncovers in what way hard it is to prithee youthful amorous wives and as well in what way alarming their baking is. He progresses techniques to heed for them in a just way. He absorbs that one spouse is a twin female sibling to a spouse of banker Gates, creating Gates his brother-in-law. Gates is in conspiration with a Las Vegas gangster, Tony Morano, whoever guarantees him that his equipped henchman Shuffles must cover interests if Gates does not.

> **After one other denizen progresses off, Gates tries to take command of the dead owner's terra firma alongside with his 2 widows (Emmanuelle Vaugier, Anita Brown) by naming in unsettled arrears. Monte is unwilling to wed up till now once more till he perceives those 2 females are very experienced in the kitchenette, consequently he stops ends up with some further acres of terra firma and 2 further wives. Monte retires the arrearage of their foremost spouse, consequently at one point more frustrating Gates, whoever pursued repossession of the mortgaged lands over quittance of the arrearage.**

Gates, irritated, has his affiliate Stewart attempt to seize Monte in the play of smoking either consuming to get him excommunicated as of the kirk and booted out of the townahip. As a celebration, Monte bears his wives for a honeymoon to Las Vegas, presenting them to gambling and different joys of the contemporary society like tennis and bikinis.

The women proceed to a women's fairness colloquy wherever the speaker, Dr. Van Dyke (Molly Shannon), preaches that females ought to control the connection and be totally identical to their slighter halves. The wives admit a strip association, one wherever males sway. Monte proceeds to get back them, wherever he stops ends up in the show.

After restoring to Utah, the women get a further authoritative part in the home and come to be fewer reliant. At the digging site for his spic-and-span ski refuge, Monte's team uncovers mortal bones and understands they have exposed an very old

Native American burying terrain.

Gates has a stratagem to outline Monte for a bogus cash working. Monte proceeds to prison, and helper Ray affirms they have certainly been constructing on an very old burying site. At a municipality case, Gates contends that Monte ought to be excommunicated. His wives and his lawyer/waiter Paul authenticate that Monte is a high-quality individual, however he is noticed culpable notwithstanding.

Tony and his right-hand individual Shuffles come in to municipality and notify Gates that they have been dispatched by felony employer Don Giovanni to bump off Monte. Gates gloats that he is of Native American descent, creating him the rightful possessor of the terra firma, activating him to spin the municipality in to a gambling refuge. Monte's wives drive a freight transporter in to the prison and split him out.

Monte races to the dig site wherever the police force show up and Gates' design is disclosed. The police force capture Gates and Monte is gratis to proceed, however Don Giovanni shows. All appears missed till Don Giovanni (Jerry Stiller) acknowledges Monte as his aged youth pal, who Monte had assembled his foremost home. Don Giovanni yells at his Hoods for not disclosing him that it was Monte sensing to construct the ski resort; else he ought to have left his high-quality pal only.

Alone with his 5 wives, Monte queries that they create a resolution regarding their time to come...leading to him acquiring flung out. Montey departs Utah however discovers pleasure with his 9th and present spouse, Dr. Van Dyke, whoever commends him for being the delicate individual she on every relevant occasion pursued.

Lex Luthor (Smallville) - Role in Smallville

Lex Luthor, instituted within Pilot (Smallville)|the pilot as the boy of billionaire Lionel Luthor (John Glover (actor)|John Glover), is dispatched to Smallville (comics)|Smallville by his dad to run the native fertilizer plant. As a kid, he is captured in the foremost Meteor shower that renders him totally smooth. Years afterward as a youthful grown-up, Lex foremost encounters Clark Kent (Tom Welling) whoever conserves his existence as of drowning and the 2 swiftly come to be acquaintances. Lex attempts to be a high-quality man for nearly all of the first seasons, however his reasons are normally moved by interest for the inexplicable, like the day Clark saved him as of drowning. As the serials unfolds, Lex goes included with different females, with altogether of the connections finishing poorly. In Smallville (season 1)|season one, he begins a connection with Victoria Hardwick (Kelly Brook), whoever was trying to employ him thus that she and her dad might purchase out LuthorCorp. Lex's way of life of bedding females and then leaving them the following day ought to seize up to him in Smallville (season 4)|season 4 once one of the females he had formerly slumbered with tries to eliminate him.

Lex has been wedded 3 periods in the show. First, in Smallville (season 2)|season 2, he wedded Desiree Atkins (Krista Allen), whoever applied her meteor-created authorities to tempt Lex in to wedding thus that she might purloin his cash. Later that season, Lex encountered and courted Characters of Smallville#Dr. Helen Bryce|Dr. Helen Bryce (Emmanuelle Vaugier) whoever ought to attempt to eliminate him on their honeymoon for rationales unidentified. In Smallville (season 6)|season 6, Lex wedded Lana Lang (Smallville)|Lana Lang (Kristin Kreuk) following beguiling her in to trusting that she was expectant with his kid. Upon educating the veracity, Lana forged her own demise and endeavored to pin the kill on Lex.

Over the program of 7 seasons—beginning in the pilot chapter on the day Clark saved him as of drowning—Lex has been attempting to expose the confidential matters that Clark retains. In season one, Lex employs Roger Nixon (Tom O'Brien (actor)|Tom O'Brien), a correspondent for the small newspaper with short articles paper The Inquisitor, to find in what way he outlived the car mishap wherever Clark preserved him as of drowning. All the proof details to Clark experiencing been hit by Lex's automobile, however Lex declines to trust that is what occured thus Nixon tries to reveal Clark to everybody. At the start of season 2, Lex executes Nixon beforehand the correspondent may eliminate Characters of Smallville#Jonathan Kent|Jonathan Kent (John Schneider (television actor)|John Schneider), whoever was safeguarding his boy as of Nixon. Lex as well enrolls the aid of Dr. Hamilton (Joe Morton) about the similar time he employs Nixon in season one; Hamilton is ordered to research the results of the Meteor rocks. Dr. Hamilton discovers an octagonal disc, with unidentified signs brand onto the disc's top that matchup these on Clark's ship, when seeking for traces of an nonnative ship that landed in Smallville in 1989. The disc is finally purloined by Nixon, whoever absorbs that it must open Clark's ship.

When Clark uncovers the Kawatche Caves in season 2, under a LuthorCorp building site, Lex chooses to come to be the conservator of the Caves to conserve them following he notes signs on the cavern enclosures that matchup the signs on the disc, as well like an octagonal form in the partition of the cavern that ought to appropriate the disc faultlessly. His attention gets bigger further and further once he discovers Clark always in the Caves, and afterward with a bit of document that shows to specify that Clark has deciphered the lingo on the cavern enclosures — though, Clark repudiates being capable to interpret the lingo. Lex's corporation, LexCorp, finally misses the Kawatche Caves to his dad Lionel, whoever has as well elaborated an attention in the Caves and the octagonal disc. Lex's interest in to the signs, and Clark, guides to a affair amid the 2 at the conclusion of Smallville (season 3)|season

3. When Lionel presents Clark a key to a area in the Luthor Mansion wherever Lex has been gathering data on Clark and his kin, Clark notifies Lex that their amity is over.

In Smallville (season 4)|season 4, Lex's awareness revolves towards detecting 3 very old stones, that hold the similar signs as these in the cavern and on the disc. He nose-dives to notice altogether 3 stones, however suspects that Clark did, and applied them to notice the prize of understanding they remained assumed to have guided to. In Smallville (season 5)|season 5, Lex goes preoccupied with uncovering Clark's secret; to this end, he breaks 3 metahuman lawbreakers out of Belle Reve and directs them to the Kent Farm, wherever they contain Lana and Clark's father and mother captive. The stratagem sums to not a thing, nevertheless, and Clark cuts Lex out of his existence totally once he discovers finds out. His interest in to the signs, that he understands to be nonnative in essence, outcomes in him being controlled by the will of the Kryptonian felonious General Zod|Zod at the conclusion of Smallville (season 5)|season 5.

It is not till Smallville (season 7)|season 7 that Lex uncovers that the signs are related to a confidential business, familiar like Veritas, that his dad is a piece of. The Veritas participants absorbed that an nonnative guest, The Traveler, ought to turn up in Smallville throughout the Meteor shower of 1989. He as well uncovers that the Veritas participants realized of a intents to command the Traveler, thus Lex places out to notice the implement. The implement, an globe he discovers in the cloak overhead a fire in the Luthor Mansion, guides Lex to the Fortress of Solitude, wherever he is challenged by Clark. At the conclusion of the 7th season, Lex utilizes the globe to carry down the Fortress about Clark and him self.

In Smallville (season 8)|season 8, Lex is lost and Characters in Smallville#Tess Mercer|Tess Mercer (Cassidy Freeman) is set in demand of LuthorCorp and its branches. She desires Lex noticed, and understands that Clark is the key to detecting him. In season eight's Bulletproof, Lana notifies Tess that she understands that Lex is alive—which Tess confirms—and that he has been holding tags on Tess by way of a nano-transmitter he in a surgical manner breed in Tess's ocular nervus opposed to her must. In the chapter Requiem, Lex utilizes Toyman|Winslow Schott to plant a Kryptonite explosive on the rooftop of the Daily Planet as a intents of holding Lana and Clark aside incessantly. As Lana took Lex's bio-enhanced suit that is developed to absorb and cast Kryptonite radioactivity, Lex drives Lana to absorb the Kryptonite to de-activate the explosive and afterward not ever be capable to proceed nearby Clark once more short of slaying him. Characters of Smallville#Oliver Queen|Oliver Queen (Justin Hartley) uncovers Lex's place and utilizes one of Schott's bombs to blow up the health conveyance Lex was journeying in, slaying him.

In the season 10 opening, it is disclosed that previous to his demise Lex had produced a numeral of replicas in an aim to employ them to cure him self. However, the major part of those replicas are faulty and age at an sped up charge. One of the replicas (Mackenzie Gray), matured about 20 annums aged compared to the actual Lex, endeavored to get vengeance on Clark however passed away beforehand he might end. In the 2-hour serials climax, it is disclosed Lex had applied the bits of different replicas to produce a perfected one; nevertheless, the duplicate lacked a heart. After a Lionel as of Multiverse (DC Comics)|an alternating actuality immolates him self to Darkseid, his heart is put inner the duplicate permitting him to live. The energized Lex talks with Clark, disclosing him he receives they have a fate as opponents, however for whichever of them to achieve their parts Clark should conquer Darkseid by stirring humankind. Lex afterward encounters with Tess, and fatally jabs her; beforehand she passes away, Tess intoxicates him with a specific neurolysin that withdraws altogether of Lex's recollections. The serials stops by moving 7 annums in to the time to come, wherever Lex has at the moment been designated President of the United States.

Absolute Deception

'Absolute Deception' (also familiar like 'Deception') is a 2013 American whodunit (genre)|thriller feature directed by Brian Trenchard-Smith, and leading Cuba Gooding, Jr. And Emmanuelle Vaugier.[http://www.goldcoast.com.au/article/2012/07/05/429311_gossip-news.html Katrina Jones, Cuba Gooding Jr shoots acts on Coast, Gold Coast Bulletin, 5 July 2012] entered 8 February 2013[http://www.variety.com/article/VR1118054203/ Diana Lodderhouse, Voltage nabs selling claims to Deception, Variety, 17 March 2012] entered 8 February 2013 The feature was disseminated on direct-to-video|direct-to-DVD in the United States on June 11, 2013.

Cerberus (film)

'Cerberus' (also familiar like 'Cerberus: the Guardian of Hell'), is a 2005 Syfy#Sci Fi Channel first films|Sci Fi Channel first feature, leading Sebastian Spence, Emmanuelle Vaugier, and Greg Evigan. The feature was managed by John Terlesky. The feature was disseminated Direct-to-video|direct–to–video in 2005.

Emmanuelle Vaugier - Film

Vaugier featured as List of Saw characters#Addison Corday|Addison in Saw II and Saw IV. In the Canadian feature Unearthed (film)|Unearthed, she played Annie, the Sheriff of a not so large bucolic barren municipality. She emerged in the feature 40 Days and 40 Nights, that featured Josh Hartnett.
She had leading parts within Suddenly Naked, in that she plays a Latin pop sensation; the TV-movie Mindstorm (film)|Mindstorm, a science-fiction thriller; and Ripper (film)|Ripper, a mental whodunit about scholars whoever cryptically vanish following enrolling in a grade about sequential assassins. She stars as well in the follow-up to Mirrors (film)|Mirrors, that is directed by Victor Garcia.Barton, Steve (March 19, 2010). [http://www.dreadcentral.com/news/36512/exclusive-mirrors-2-hit-home-video Exclusive: Mirrors 2 to Hit Home Video on ...]. Dread Central.com. Retrieved March 20, 2010.

Maxim (magazine)|Maxim periodical highlighted her on the cover of the February 2006 subject in the United States. Three months afterward, she landed mark #31 on their yearly Hot 100 catalog.[http://www.maxim.com/amg/girls/articles/92045/2006-hot-100.html Maxim Girls: 2006 Hot 100]. (May 1, 2006). Maxim (magazine)|Maxim. Retrieved May 20, 2011.[http://www.emmanuellevaugier.com/press/Maxim_100.htm 31ndash;Emmanuelle Vaugier]. Maxim (magazine)|Maxim. Retrieved May 20, 2011.

Secondhand Lions - Cast

* Haley Joel Osment as Walter Caldwell
* Robert Duvall as Hub McCann
* Michael Caine as Garth McCann
* Kyra Sedgwick as Mae Caldwell
* Nicky Katt as Stan
* Josh Lucas as Adult Walter Caldwell
* Michael O'Neill (actor)|Michael O'Neill as Ralph
* Deirdre O'Connell (actress)|Deirdre O'Connell as Helen
* Christian Kane as Young Hub
* Daniel Brooks as Sheik's Great-Grandson
* Kevin Haberer as Young Garth
* Eric Balfour as Sheik's grandson
* **Emmanuelle Vaugier as Jasmine**
* Adam Ozturk as The Sheik
* Adrian Pasdar as Skeet Machine Salesman, also known as clay chump launcher
* Mitchel Musso as Boy

* Marc Musso as Boy
* Jennifer Stone as Martha
* as Jasmine the Lion
* Billy Joe Shaver as conveyance freight transporter driver

Ripper (film) - Plot

Molly Keller (A. J. Cook (actress)|A. J. Cook), scarcely fails being killed by a sequential assassin, following running to get away an isle. Five annums afterward, she bears a forensic psychological science grade as of well known specialist Marshall Kane (Bruce Payne). Also in the grade are Jason Korda (Ryan Northcott), Chantal Etienne (Claire Keim), Marisa Tavares (Kelly Brook), Eddie Sackman (Derek Hamilton), Mary-Anne Nordstrom (Daniella Evangelista), Andrea Carter (Emmanuelle Vaugier) and Aaron Kroeker (Courtney J. Stevens). During a grade, Marshall pranks his grade by professing to kill one of the scholars, to display anybody might be a assassin. After grade, Aaron divulges he understands regarding Molly's bygones, that antagonizes her as she does not desire to address about her bygones. Eddie strikes on Molly, however she discards him.

At nighttime, the cluster, excepting Aaron, encounter for a research meeting, nevertheless have an argumentation over Molly's unfriendly stance. They choose to proceed to a party seizing place in an deserted constructing. Jason tries to get to comprehend Molly, however she stays far-off. Meanwhile, Marisa has intercourse with a masked individual, beforehand she perceives Chantal and Andrea conversing regarding her. Marisa chooses to leave, however is taken up to an separated floor of the constructing by the lift. She is shortly striked and stabbed by the assassin, beforehand she drops out a window. A catena, enveloped about her ankle joint, latches her, however the assassin hoists her back up and jabs her to demise, beforehand dispatching her form crashing via a window in to the party beneath.

The following day, the cluster agonize Marisa's demise, when determining they tend to attempt and recognize whoever the assassin is. Molly encounters Detective Kelso (Jürgen Prochnow), whoever was piece of the examination of the foregoing homicides. The couple proceed to the kill set wherever Detective Kelso alerts Molly that he understands the assassin is back. Mary-Anne is powering home to perceive her kin once a black freight transporter starts to RAM in to the back of her automobile. She tries to drive off, however the freight transporter drives her to the aspect of a precipice. As she tries to get out, the freight transporter strikes her automobile once more, bringing about her to smash via the windscreen and crash to her demise. Detective Kelso discovers her form in a closeby shed, wherever the assassin has stabbed her frequently.

Molly tests Marshall, and displays the assassin is ensuing the design of the well known sequential assassin Jack the Ripper. Jason organizes to coax the cluster to resume researching notwithstanding their distrust. Molly and Jason find a killer formerly held Marshall captive. Chantal smooches Jason, however shortly apologises to Molly for undertaking thus, and the couple create acquaintances. While Andrea is at the Morgue recognizing Mary-Anne's lesions, she is followed by the assassin whoever narcotics her beforehand gutting her.

Jason, Chantal, and Eddie notice find out about Molly's bygones, that triggers an argumentation ensuing in Molly eliminating herself as of the cluster. An sad Molly is comforted by Marshall. The ensuing nighttime, Molly, Jason, Eddie, Chantal, and Marshall are taken to a cottage wherever they understand the sufferers share the similar initials of the sufferers of Jack the Ripper. Suspicion drops on Aaron, whoever was the one that constructed the research cluster. They aim to telephone Detective Kelso, however the telephone is not functioning. After Molly and Chantal fall out, Eddie, Jason, and Chantal leave to attempt and mend the telephone orbiter on top of the alp. Their automobile shortly breaks down, making Jason to take on on base. Eddie tries to mend the automobile, when Chantal stays inner. The assassin shortly shows and thumps out Chantal beforehand Eddie's hand is confined inner the Hood (vehicle)|bonnet of the automobile. Chantal wakens up and panics, powering the automobile onward in to a tree, slaying Eddie following his back is squashed by the tree that Chantal smashed in to . The assassin pursuings Chantal to a plant, wherever she coincidentally activates a record breaking engine. She bumps in to Aaron whoever alerts her he understands whoever the assassin is. She attempts to get away, however they fall in to the engine, wherever they are either mangled by the round saws.

Back at the cottage, Molly goes dubious of either Jason and Marshall. As Jason comes back, Molly thumps him out beforehand operating in to the woods. She experiences Jason once more and escapes when the assassin hacks him to demise with an axe. Molly uncovers Marshall positioning over a killed Jason, beforehand Detective Kelso comes and thumps out Marshall. Molly additionally hallucinates and perceives her junior ego in the woods, gesturing to the 2 males and proposing that Molly is the one whoever slayed them altogether. Later, Marshall is carried out for the homicides, and expected to noticeable psychological difficulties, Molly is set in an mad asylum.

It has been indicated that the assassin was not ever definitively designated within the feature, and there is proposal that Detective Kelso is really the assassin. During the beginning kill set, as the youthful Molly flees on a vessel, she jabs the assassin in the hand when he tries to ascend on to the vessel following her. Detective Kelso is noticed in any set in the film to be wearing solely one concertedly on the similar hand that the assassin was stabbed in.

Dolan's Cadillac (film)

'Dolan's Cadillac' is a 2009 Thriller (genre)|thriller leading Wes Bentley, Christian Slater and Emmanuelle Vaugier.[http://www.worstpreviews.com/headline.php?id=13527 Christian Slater in Stephen King's Dolan's Cadillac] It is founded on a Dolan's Cadillac|short tale of the similar designation by Stephen King.[http://shocktillyoudrop.com/news/topnews.php?id=13726 Stephen King Adaptation Drives Direct-to-DVD]

Painkiller Jane (film) - Plot

A Special Forces component, familiar like the Painkiller Unit, is revealed to a biochemical armament when on a assignment in Sovetskaia, Chechnya. After trying to withdraw, the whole component is ambushed and carried out by a cluster of equipped males in careful hazmat suits. One associate of the component, Captain Jane Browning (Emmanuelle Vaugier), not solely stays alive the implementation, however recovers as of the virus-related contagion, and progresses an abnormally quick healing reason, expanded adroitness, pace, potency, increased senses, psychological capabilities and a pictorial retention. Her senses accelerate to take in and procedure data at a hyper-normal charge, and her intellect reorganizes what she has noticed in to systematical reasoning, such like plotting out a chess game and Recognizing models In the sort of a periodical item.

She is taken to a US Army research lab wherever experts in science are attempting to absorb what occured thus they may produce an military of super-soldiers. The head scientist whoever is serving to notice find out wherefore she outlived and altered once the other ones passed away is Dr. Graham Knight. She is informed by Col. Ian Watts, her adviser, that the virus was generated by a biochemical extremist designated Peter Erfan whoever has a mastermind IQ. As the US Army is conveying her to one other center in Alaska, Knight progresses her a record indicating that they are not ever going to let her proceed. Jane flees in an attempt to notice Peter Erfan and obtain vengeance on him for murdering her group. She proceeds to the Uni for aid as of Dr. Knight, however discovers that Dr. Knight is not the individual whoever was functioning with her at the military center.

As she challenges the individual she realized as Doctor Knight at his guesthouse, he divulges that he is Captain Lucas Hensley and is with army intellect. He is covert and researching her senior official, Col. Ian Watts. Hensley informs her that Watts generated Erfan and applied him as the faultless cover. Since Erfan did not subsist additionally he could not be captured. Hensley queries Jane to aid seize him. She proceeds to challenge Watts herself, however like she does thus, they are either shot by an unidentified murderer. As she is attempting to hold the seeping on Watts, a few of her blood drops in to his lesion and mixes with his blood. It is suggested that this might have permitted the lieutenant colonel to recuperate as of being shot.

She proceeds following the shooter and he guides her to Lucas Hensley. Hensley confesses that he is in reality Peter Erfan and has a ampoule of fluid that he has taken out as of Jane. As he is conversing with her the murderer begins to turn in on her and she shoots him. Erfan alludes to her as the spic-and-span Eve, as somewhat in her form changed the virus and then the virus altered her. This is wherefore she outlived however the rest of her component did not. Erfan has been capable to recreate this altered infectious agent and previously gave it to the murderer. As he is conversing with her the murderer that was shot receives up and rips off a power container on the partition and strikes Jane in the head with it.

The following set Erfan has her shackled in a chopper and is seizing her off. She breaks out of the Handcuffs and begins battling with Erfan. Shots are dismissed in to the console of the chopper and the murderer, whoever is navigating, misses command of the chopper. This triggers Erfan and Jane to fall out of the chopper and they grapple with every one other when dropping towards the H2O beneath. The following set perceives Col. Watts in a boneyard wherever he is positioning over her gravestone. He additionally proceeds to the abbreviate and receives on a vessel. There he encounters Jane and presents her a spic-and-span ID and cash. She sails off in the vessel.

The ultimate set perceives a cluster of Asian grandee strolling in to a research lab and encounter with Lucas Hensley whoever evidently outlived the fall uninjured. He contains a ampoule of green flowing, the hereditary matter for the improvement infectious agent in resolution. The connection is that Erfan took the serum him self, in line to endure the influence with watercourse and he must shortly be generating an military of superhumans for the unnamed Asian trade collaborator.

Ripper (film) - Cast

* A. J. Cook (actress)|A. J. Cook like Molly Keller
* Bruce Payne as Marshall Kane
* Ryan Northcott as Jason Korda
* Claire Keim as Chantal Etienne

* Kelly Brook as Marisa Tavares
* Derek Hamilton as Eddie Sackman
* Daniella Evangelista as Mary-Anne Nordstrom
* **Emmanuelle Vaugier as Andrea Carter**
* Jürgen Prochnow as Detective Kelso
* Courtenay J. Stevens as Aaron Kroeker
* Dominika Wolski as Kissing Blonde/Grinding Girl

Human Target (2010 TV series) - Recurring characters

* **Emmanuelle Vaugier as FBI Special Agent Emma Barnes – following her vocation was tarnished by Chance's doings in Embassy Row, Chance is capable to get her aid to halt Baptiste's murder assignment in Baptiste. With Baptiste's capture, Barnes' standing is suggested to have been reinstated. Barnes and Chance have obfuscated amorous emotions for every one other.**
* Autumn Reeser as Layla – a computer specialist whoever was originally functioning for a dishonest protection servicer corporation Sentronics in Lockdown, however following it was destroyed by Chance, Layla was enlisted to freelance for the group in Baptiste.
* Leonor Varela as Maria Gallego – Chance's erstwhile sweetheart whoever queries for his aid in Salvage Reclamation. They are reunified at one point more in A Problem Like Maria once she queries for his help once more to save a pal of hers. She is as well disclosed to be wedded, a confidential she retains as of him till they share their goodbyes.
* Lennie James as Baptiste – an murderer engaged by The Old Man whoever formerly operated with Chance, being his collaborator, scholar and pal. Baptiste is one of the world's largest assassins; unprincipled, merciless, unbelievably effectual and lethal, however he owes altogether his expertises to being instructed by Chance. Baptiste did not take it well once Chance ran off, and even at the moment fights to comprehend. Baptiste is accountable for countless demises, containing the perfect strikes of crowns of state. Most especially, Baptiste slayed Katherine Walters and the foregoing Christopher Chance as noticed in Christopher Chance. Baptiste's design to annihilate Operation Olive Branch, a confidential UN tranquility top, was foiled by Chance and Agent Barnes, and thus Baptiste was taken in to care by the FBI in Baptiste. The Return of Baptiste displays that he was moved to a Russian Gulag. He exposed Chance following being enlisted to aid the group in recovering captives taken by Don Miguel Cervantes. Baptiste queries to come to be Cervantes' head agreement assassin, beforehand exposing Cervantes to retain Chance. On restoring as of the assignment Baptiste oaths not ever to dispersed to the Russian Gulag as guaranteed, however he is outsmarted by Chance up till now once more.

He is as well presented to gather his victims' watches.
* Armand Assante as The Old Man – the guider of an business of non-amateur soldiers of fortune and assassins, his 2 best-loved juniors remained Chance and Baptiste however, when he respects them either similarly, he contemplated Chance his best-loved and, getting to be a substitute father-figure to him, groomed him to be his replacement, to the point he gave him his personal designation like Chance's - and once Chance ran and vanished, seizing the designation Christopher Chance, it was indicated to have broken his heart. He searches for to re-recruit Chance back in to his business. His standing for ruthlessness is thus significant Chance welcomed the Old Man was the one individual he is frightened of.
* Tony Hale as Harry – a undisclosed inspector whoever helps Chance and the group.

Cerberus (film) - Cast

*Sebastian Spence as Jake Addams
***Emmanuelle Vaugier as Dr. Samantha Gaines**
*Greg Evigan as Marcus Cutter
*Garret Sato as Kul Jae Sung
*Brent Florence as Zach Gaines
*Michael Cory Davis as Burke
*KB Nau as Knipstrom
*Chuck Caudill Jr. As Reinholdt
*Bogdan Uritescu as Max
*Gelu Nitu as Radu
*Catalin Paraschiv as Dorsey
*Gabi Andronache as Attila the Hun

Mr. Monk Gets Jury Duty - Production

The chapter holds one of the greatest visitor casts in the show's history; this is in piece expected to the directing of an whole jury. Carlos Gómez (actor)|Carlos Gómez was cast in the part of Miguel Escobar, a desired escapee whoever was captured first in the chapter. The jury contained, in line of juryman numeral, Bonita Friedericy, David Ackert, Carlease Burke, Wings Hauser, Bryan Coffee, Kimi Reichenberg, Benito Martinez (actor)|Benito Martinez, unidentified, Van Epperson, Kevin Bernsten, Tony Shalhoub, and Emmanuelle Vaugier. Many of those visitors ought to afterward proceed on to have greater parts within different displays, containing Friedericy on Chuck (TV series)|Chuck and Vaugier on Covert Affairs. This is author Peter Wolk's second chapter, following authoring Monk (season 3)|season three's Mr. Monk Gets Fired (3.04). Wolk,

whoever formerly operated like a felonious protection lawyer, had as well authored court-room chapters for the displays The Defenders (1997 TV series)|The Defenders and Fighting the Odds. The tale was authored by Wolk, alongside with Andy Breckman, Tom Scharpling, David Breckman, Joe Toplyn, Dan Dratch, and Hy Conrad over a 7 days in 2005 in Summit, New Jersey. It is director Andrei Belgrader's 4th, following directing Mr. Monk Gets Fired (3.04), Mr. Monk and the Kid (3.16), and Mr. Monk Gets Drunk (4.05). The chapter was shot in Los Angeles, aside as of the beginning Chinatown pursuit set, as Stottlemeyer and Disher pursuit Escobar up Jackson Street, that was shot on-location in November 2005 in San Francisco. Because of the occasion to feature on-location, the beginning set was re-written. The jury subplot deeply parodies the timeless feature 12 Angry Men (1957 film)|12 Angry Men. These contain a sole opening not culpable ballot and the similar sort of brand applied to effect either offenses. Many jurors are counterparts of these in 12 Angry Men, containing Patel (David Ackert) and Juror #11 (Jiří Voskovec|George Voskovec), whoever are newcomers pleased to be in America; Mr. Cobb (Wings Hauser) and Juror #3 (Lee J. Cobb), whoever are every one adversaries and the final to ballot not culpable (interestingly, either the Monk type and the 12 Angry Men performer are either designated Mr. Cobb); the athletics fan juryman (Kevin Bernsten) and Juror #7 (Jack Warden), whoever either create different baseball game references; and Monk analogues Juror #8 (Henry Fonda), the solitary opening not culpable ballots. Additionally, the sifting shot of the jury area was motivated by an indistinguishable shot towards the conclusion of 12 Angry Men. Wolk authored that the authoring group observed the features 12 Angry Men and Jury Duty (film)|Jury Duty over the program of manufacture.

Bachelor Party 2: The Last Temptation - Cast

As billed,http://www.imdb.com/title/tt0954541/ the cast as well contains
Greg Pitts,
Harland Williams,
Warren Christie,
Danny A. Jacobs,
Max Landwirth,
Emmanuelle Vaugier,
Karen-Eileen Gordon,
Mauricio Sanchez,
Steve Crowley|Steven Crowley, and
Audrey Landers.

Blonde and Blonder

'Blonde and Blonder' is a 2008 Canadian farce feature leading Pamela Anderson, Denise Richards and Emmanuelle Vaugier. The feature was managed by Dean Hamilton, and was disseminated on January 18, 2008.

The film's designation is a mention to Dumb and Dumber.

Covert Affairs - Recurring cast

* Eion Bailey as 'Ben Mercer' (season 1–2): Annie's former boyfriend, whoever was being earmarked by the CIA, beforehand restoring to the Agency. He is employed by Arthur as a black Ops go-between.
* Gregory Itzin as 'Henry Wilcox' (season 1–4): the erstwhile CIA Director of the National Clandestine Service; Jai Wilcox's dad. Henry afterward goes the principal adversary in season 4 and is slayed by Annie in the season climax.
* Oded Fehr as 'Eyal Lavin' (season 1–present): a Mossad worker whoever sometimes functions with Annie on her assignments. By the conclusion of season 3 Eyal departs Mossad however resumes to aid Annie out on her assignments.
* Noam Jenkins as 'Vincent Rossabi' (season 1–present): an FBI go-between with who Annie should sometimes work notwithstanding their hostile connection.
* Sarah Clarke as 'Lena Smith' (season 3): Annie's manager in one other CIA division. Lena is not pleased with Annie's execution and directs Annie back to the DPD. Lena understands in a further hands-on, straight activity style to spying as contrasted to Joan's by-the-book style. She is slayed by Annie once disclosed to be a traitor.
* **Emmanuelle Vaugier as 'Liza Hearn' (season 1–2): a correspondent with a strange origin inner the CIA, whoever expected to issue a serials of causing damage items regarding the Agency.**
* Richard Coyle as 'Simon Fischer' (season 3): A undertaking financier, and distrusted FSB (Russia)|FSB snoop, who Annie is allocated to cultivate when functioning in Lena's division throughout season 3. Simon afterward drops in fancy with Annie and designs to run off with her. He is afterward slayed by Lena.

Gordon family (Saw) - Addison Corday

* **Portrayed by Emmanuelle Vaugier**
* Appears in: Saw II, Saw IV, Saw V
* Status: Deceased (Saw II)

Addison is a call girl, and a casualty in the Saw II|Nerve Gas House. Like the other sufferers, she was framed by Detective Eric Matthews (Saw)|Eric Matthews. She tries to work with the other captives to endure, however on educating that one other casualty, #Daniel Matthews|Daniel is Eric Matthews' boy, she starts functioning only to notice an cure. She extends in to a glass container to get back an cure, and her arms get captured in the razor edged arm sockets. Xavier discovers her, however departs her to bleed to demise following perusing the numeral on the back of her nape. In Saw IV, she is noticed in a flashback, contributing John her facilities, previous to John getting to be the Jigsaw Killer, and in a flashback in Saw V reposing knocked out as John and Hoffman set up the Nerve Gas House. According to the Saw II internet site, Addison is authored to be 29 annums aged.

Saw II

'Saw II' is a 2005 Canadian-American terror feature, a follow-up to 2004's Saw (2004 film)|Saw and the second part within the seven-part Saw (franchise)|Saw enfranchisement, directed and co-written by Darren Lynn Bousman. Co-written with serials maker Leigh Whannell whoever authored and featured in the foremost feature, it stars Donnie Wahlberg, Franky G, Glenn Plummer, Beverley Mitchell, Dina Meyer, Emmanuelle Vaugier, Erik Knudsen, with Shawnee Smith, and Tobin Bell. Smith, Bell and Meyer are the solely performers to repeat their parts as of the foremost feature.

The feature attributes Jigsaw (Saw franchise)|Jigsaw being arrested by the police force, however trapping the detaining official in one of his personal diversions when displaying one other game of 8 folks — containing the officer's boy — in advance on TV screens at one other place. It as well investigates a few of Jigsaw's backstory, delivering a limited clarification of his cause for getting to be Jigsaw.

After the monetary triumph of Saw, a follow-up was right away green-lit. Leigh Whannell and James Wan remained occupied planning for their following feature and remained incapable to record either straight. Bousman authored a text named The Desperate beforehand Saw was disseminated and was sensing for a maker however numerous studios refused it. Hoffman experienced the text and presented it to his associates Mark Burg and Oren Koules. It was determined that, with a few amends, it might be produced in to Saw II. Whannell grew to be accessible to supply re-writes of the text. The feature was specified a greater financial plan and was shot as of May to June 2005 in Toronto.

Saw II was disseminated on October 28, 2005 and, notwithstanding pessimistic appraisals as of reviewers, was a monetary triumph, with beginning takings of $31.9 million and earning $88 million in the United States and Canada. It has stayed the biggest earning Saw feature in these nations. Bell was proposed for Best Villain at the 2006 MTV Movie Awards for his part as Jigsaw in the feature. Saw II was disseminated to DVD on and exceeded graphs its foremost 7 days, vending further compared to 3 million units. At the time, it was the fastest-selling dramatic DVD in Lionsgate's past.

The Beach Boys: An American Family - Cast

*Kevin Dunn as Murry Wilson
*Fred Weller as Brian Wilson
*Alley Mills as Audree Wilson
*Nick Stabile as Dennis Wilson
***Emmanuelle Vaugier as Suzanne Love**
*Ryan Northcott as Carl Wilson
*Matt Letscher as Mike Love
*Ned Vaughn as Al Jardine
*Dublin James as David Marks (musician)|David Marks
*Jesse Caron as Bruce Johnston
*Amy Van Horne as Marilyn Rovell
*Jad Mager as Nick Venet
*Eric Matheny as Chuck Britz
*Harris Laskaway as Voyle Gilmore
*Clay Wilcox as Tommy Schaeffer
*Anthony Rapp as Van Dyke Parks
*Erik Passoja as Charles Manson
*David Polcyn as Phil Spector
*Tera Hendrickson as Carol Kaye
*James Intveld as Hal Blaine
*Jessica Shannon as a musical performance girl
*Elliot Kendall as Glen Campbell
*Steve Stanley as Barney Kessel
*Trevor St. John as Jan Berry
*Jacob Young like Dean Torrence

Mirrors 2 - Plot

Max Matheson (Nick Stahl) is included in a automobile mishap that executes his betrothed, Kayla (Jennifer Sipes). Due to the mishap, he goes weepy bothered and undergoes mental care with Dr. Beaumont (Ann Mckenzie), creating a few advance in transacting with the culpability over the mishap. To aid Max turn onward, his dad, Jack Matheson (William Katt), reopens the Mayflower Department Store in New Orleans, Louisiana|New Orleans and asks Max to substitute the safeguarding watch, whoever not long ago exit under strange situations when evidently Self-harm|cutting him self up on work.

Max receives the assignment and his dad presents him to the store administrator, Keller Landreaux (Lawrence Turner), the customer, Jenna McCarty (Christy Carlson Romano|Christy Romano), and the vice-president of transactions, Ryan Parker (Jon Michael Davis). Before his foremost move, Max perceives a apparition of a lamented female in a reflect, and then perceives Jenna's reflection, ripping off her head. Meanwhile, Jenna is slayed by her reflection, being flung via glass entrances and a sliver of glass decapitating her. Max registers that he foresees the demises within the reflects. That nighttime, he attempts to notice the apparition, however in lieu perceives Ryan's reflection being Disembowelment|eviscerated. He attempts to interaction Ryan, however receives no reply. Later, Ryan is slayed, in the similar means like his reflection.

Max perceives his father's face concealed in cuts in a billabong additionally races to his father's home. Jack is nearly slayed by his reflection, following Max produced it to his home and clues to whoever is manipulating the reflects that he ought to do whatsoever she desires him to undertake if she spares his dad. Max afterward returns to the Mayflower, however he is halted by Detectives Huston and Piccirilli (Lance E. Nichols, Wayne Pére), clarifying about what occured in Ryan and Jenna's demises. Max repudiates whatever participation and, although they stay dubious, they let Max get back to his work.

> **Max proceeds to the principal reflect, to notice find out whoever the apparition is. Suddenly, Max's reflection displays a light, that Max tails in every one of the reflects. He discovers a container and opens it to notice an ID of a female designated Eleanor Reigns (Stephanie Honoré|Stephanie Honoré Sanchez), a spic-and-span worker of the Mayflower whoever vanished 2 months before. The light shines external and Max discovers a lost individual adventure for Eleanor. Max peruses it like he connections Eleanor's aged female sibling Elizabeth (Emmanuelle Vaugier) to absorb particulars of her vanishing. Together, they find that somebody had removed the observation files on the nighttime of Eleanor's vanishing in the store's computer.**

Max and Elizabeth sojourn Henry Schow (Evan Jones), the store's erstwhile safeguarding watch and the final individual whoever entered the files. Henry's mouth had been scarred by his reflection. Through Henry, they absorb that Eleanor is lamented and her will is attempting to find vengeance on whoever was included in her kill.

Two months previous, throughout the Mayflower's magnificent beginning party, Jenna and Ryan spiked Eleanor's sip with narcotics. Keller raped Eleanor when she was besotted and was immediately accountable for her demise. Henry noticed Keller entombing Eleanor's form in Mayflower's basement's crawlspace and is ordered to remove the observation files to cover up the felony. Two days following her demise, Eleanor, whose psyche is confined in the reflect society, started stalking them. She started to mutilate Henry by manipulating his reflection to consume shards of glass following he removed the files, and finally slayed Jenna and Ryan, beforehand moving on to Keller. When Eleanor registered that Max might perceive her, she enforced him to aid her create interaction with her female sibling by alarming his father's existence. Max registers that his Near-Death encounter a annum previous has specified him an capacity to perceive the Afterlife|other aspect.

Max and Elizabeth proceed to the Mayflower and seek for Eleanor's form in its cellar. They are pursued by Keller, following he registers that they comprehend what occured. He almost strangles Elizabeth, however Max conserves her, consequently duplicating the Near-Death experience Max had accomplished and permitting Elizabeth to perceive Eleanor. After identifying Eleanor once more, Max wrestles Keller, thrusting him to the principal reflect. Eleanor executes Keller, saving Max and Elizabeth, however leaving them in shock. At the police force facility, Henry admits to the detectives of his accidental participation in Eleanor's kill. The police force examination room's one-way reflect begins to crack following Henry is only, and he perceives Eleanor once more on its reflection. Henry's hoot is perceived following the screen cuts to black.

Absolute Deception - Cast

* Cuba Gooding, Jr. As John Nelson
* **Emmanuelle Vaugier as Rebecca Scott**
* Evert McQueen as Inspector Hendricks
* Ty Hungerford as Archer
* Jeff Gannon as D.A. Cochran
* Brad McMurray as Thug #1
* Kelly Atkinson as Brigid Archer
* Sean Edward Frazer as Police Officer #1
* Troy MacKinder as Associate
* Raymond Massey as Coroner
* Rachel Morgan-McMurray as New Yorker

* Gulliver Page as Thug #2
* Candice Storey as Constable Jill Davis
* Sam White as Police Officer #2

Call Me: The Rise and Fall of Heidi Fleiss (film) - Cast

* Jamie-Lynn Sigler as Heidi Fleiss
* Brenda Fricker as Madame Alex
* Saul Rubinek as Paul Fleiss
* **Emmanuelle Vaugier as Lauren**
* Natassia Malthe as Charisse
* Ian Tracey as Sergeant Willeford
* Blu Mankuma as Police chief
* Robert Davi as Ivan Nagy
* Corbin Bernsen as Steve
* Hrant Alianak as Prince Hassan
* Crystal Balint as Tracey
* Susannah Hoffmann as Elissa Fleiss
* Missy Peregrym as Tina
* Joe Norman Shaw as Heidi's Lawyer
* Stefanie Von Pfetten as Michelle

List of Saw characters - Addison Corday

* **Portrayed by Emmanuelle Vaugier**
* Appears in: Saw II, Saw IV, Saw V

Addison is a call girl, and a casualty in the Saw II|Nerve Gas House. Like the other sufferers, she was framed by Detective Eric Matthews (Saw)|Eric Matthews. She tries to work with the other captives to endure, however on educating that one other casualty, #Daniel Matthew's|Daniel, is Eric Matthews' boy, she starts functioning only to notice an cure. She extends in to a glass container to get back an cure, and her arms get captured in the razor edged arm sockets. Xavier discovers her, however departs her to bleed to demise following perusing the numeral on the back of her nape. In Saw IV, she is noticed in a flashback, contributing John her facilities, previous to John getting to be the Jigsaw Killer,and in a flashback in Saw V reposing knocked out as John and Hoffman set up the Nerve Gas House. According to the Saw II internet site, Addison is authored to be 29 annums aged.

Saw II - Cast

* Tobin Bell as Jigsaw (Saw)|John Kramer
* Shawnee Smith as Amanda Young
* Donnie Wahlberg as Eric Matthews (Saw)|Detective Eric Matthews
* Erik Knudsen as List of Saw characters#Daniel Matthews|Daniel Matthews
* Franky G as List of Saw characters#Xavier Chavez|Xavier Chavez
* Dina Meyer as List of Saw characters#Allison Kerry|Detective Allison Kerry
* Lyriq Bent as List of Saw characters#Daniel Rigg|Sergeant Daniel Rigg
* Glenn Plummer as List of Saw characters#Jonas Singer|Jonas Singer
* Beverly Mitchell as List of Saw characters#Laura Hunter|Laura Hunter

*** Emmanuelle Vaugier as List of Saw characters#Addison Corday|Addison Corday**

* Timothy Burd as List of Saw characters#Obi Tate|Obi Tate
* Tony Nappo as List of Saw characters#Gus Colyard|Gus Colyard
* Noam Jenkins as List of Saw characters#Michael Marks|Michael Marks

Covert Affairs - Development, casting, and production

Covert Affairs foremost emerged on USA Network's creation slate in July 2008. The pilot chapter was authored by Matt Corman and Chris Ord. Casting was afoot in June 2009, with the anticipation that prosperous directing ought to head to a manufacture responsibility. Piper Perabo was the foremost female actor cast in first July 2009, as CIA official Annie Walker. The directing of Christopher Gorham appeared in belated July, swiftly pursued by an statement that the pilot had been allowed by USA Network.

In first August 2009, Tim Matheson signed on to manage a 90-minute pilot. Further directing statements contained Anne Dudek in mid-August, pursued by Kari Matchett and Peter Gallagher in first September. Eric Lively was cast as a companion CIA official and peer to Perabo's type, and Eion Bailey was cast in a repeating part as Perabo's former boyfriend. The pilot started shooting in Toronto in September 2009.

In January 2010, the Covert Affairs pilot experienced a 10-episodes direction. Sendhil Ramamurthy was appended to the cast as a CIA official, substituting Lively's type, alongside with Emmanuelle Vaugier in a repeating part as a correspondent.

The serials head creators are Doug Liman and David Bartis and the co-executive maker is Jonathan Glassner.[http://www.imdb.com/name/nm0322106/news#ni3113561 IMDb on executives] The show expresses on July 13 (10/9 C) Executive created by Doug Liman and David Bartis, Jonathan Glassner (Co-executive producer). A New Series From the Producers of Mr. Mrs. Smith" and the Producer of the Bourne Trilogy... Production of the serials bears place in Toronto, Ontario, at main fixed places accommodated in a workshop, as well like at merchandise shooting places all over the native zone. This is rolled into one with matter shot at different global places within that the series' chapters are set, such like Washington, D.C., seizing topographically distinctive components of those emplaces. In a few cases, the series' creators employ a stand-in place for shots wherever the outlays and provisioning of the real place shoot are not practical, either if the place stated is fictitious.

The second season started shooting in March, 2011.

40 Days and 40 Nights - Cast

* Josh Hartnett as Matt Sullivan
* Shannyn Sossamon as Erica Sutton
* Paulo Costanzo as Ryan
* Maggie Gyllenhaal as Sam
* Vinessa Shaw as Nicole
* Adam Trese as John Sullivan
* Griffin Dunne as Jerry Anderson
* Keegan Connor Tracy as Mandy
* **Emmanuelle Vaugier as Susie**
* Monet Mazur as Candy
* Christine Chatelain as Andie
* Stanley Anderson as Father Maher
* Lorin Heath as Diana
* Glenn Fitzgerald as Chris
* Jarrad Paul as Duncan
* Terry Chen as Neil
* Kai Lennox as Nick
* Chris Gauthier as Mikey
* Barry Newman as Walter Sullivan
* Mary Gross as Bev Sullivan
* Dylan Neal as David Brokaw

CPSIA information can be obtained at www.ICGtesting.com
Printed in the USA
LVOW03s0230121114

413139LV00017B/147/P